QUALITYREVIEWER

Appraising the design quality of development proposals

Qualityreviewer is a method that helps planners, councillors, developers, planning applicants and others who shape places to appraise design quality.

Qualityreviewer can:

- Structure pre-application discussions, focusing on quality at the start and helping planners and applicants to understand one another
- Structure design statements, focusing them on the important issues
- Structure planning applications
- Provide a clear and simple basis for appraising the design quality of planning applications

Part A presents the Qualityreviewer method concisely (pages 11-29), and in a two-page summary (pages 30-31). Part B provides a guide to thinking about design quality. Part C shows the place of Qualityreviewer in the planning process.

Published by Thomas Telford Limited, 40 Marsh Wall, London E14 9TP, UK.
www.thomastelford.com

Distributors for Thomas Telford books are
Australia: DA Books and Journals, 648 Whitehorse Road, Mitcham 3132, Victoria

First published 2010

Also available from Thomas Telford Limited
Manual for streets. Department for Transport, Communities and Local Government, Welsh Assembly Government. ISBN: 978-0-7277-3501-0
Design and access statements explained. R. Cowan. ISBN: 978-0-7277-3440-2
Graphics for urban design. B. Meeda, N. Parkyn and D. S. Walton. ISBN: 978-0-7277-3399-3

www.icevirtuallibrary.com

A catalogue record for this book is available from the British Library

ISBN: 978-0-7277-4057-1

Designed by Draught Associates, London
Printed and bound in Great Britain by Latimer Trend & Company Ltd., Plymouth

Authors
Rob Cowan, Scott Adams and David Chapman are directors of Urban Design Skills (www.urbandesignskills.com).
Rob Cowan's previous publications include the CLG/CABE's *By Design* (joint author), the Scottish Government's *Designing Places* and *The Dictionary of Urbanism*.

Acknowledgements
Thanks are due to Nathan Blanchard, Sarah Cary, Dave Chetwyn, Arthur Clarke, Tim Cronin, Carole-Anne Davies, Georges Droogmans, Sophie Duke, Paul Evans, Helen Forman, Kayla Friedman, Gerry Grams, Tamsin Hart, Kelvin Hinton, Robert Huxford, Anthony Keown, Diarmaid Lawlor, Simon Leask, Alan Mace, Riccardo Marini, Luke McDonald, Daniel McKendry, Angelique Najab-Antoine, Laura O'Dea, John Punter, Barry Sellers, Julia Smachylo, Robert Smith, Frank Stocks, Deb Upadhyaya, Atam Verdi, Julia Wallace, Jack Warshaw, Chris Watts and David Wheeler.

Note
This book does not state the names of most of the architects and other designers of the buildings and places it illustrates. Responsibility for a development's success or failure is a complex business. Most development is designed by members of several different professions working in collaboration. Its quality may also be determined by a number of other people, not necessarily designers or professionals, who are involved in the planning and development process, and who may set expectations and determine what is possible.

www.qualityreviewer.co.uk

Front cover
A street at Newhall in Harlow, Essex. Street trees help to give the message that car movement does not take priority over other uses in the public space. The master plan for this major development was drawn up after the landowners decided that they wanted to achieve a much higher quality of design than was usual for housing in that area. Illustration by Rob Cowan.

Contents

*'**Quality** of place matters in many ways. There are few things that we want for ourselves, our families or our country that are not affected by the built environment. Bad planning and design and careless maintenance encourages crime, contributes to poor health, undermines community cohesion, deters investment, spoils the environment and, over the long term, incurs significant costs.'*
World Class Places, Communities and Local Government (2009)

*'Good design is indivisible from good planning. Planning authorities should plan positively for the achievement of high **quality** and inclusive design for all development.'*
Planning Policy Statement 1: Delivering Sustainable Development (2005)

*'Poorly-designed developments in unsuitable places can damage the **quality** of life in a community. The quality, location and environmental impact of any new development always need careful consideration.'*
Scottish Government (2009)

*'Good design can protect the environment and enhance its **quality**, help to attract business and investment, promote social inclusion and improve the quality of life.'*
Planning Policy Wales, Welsh Assembly Government (2002)

*'The **quality** of where we live depends not just on the design of buildings, but on their layout and landscaping, the arrangements made for access and, in particular, how they relate to their surroundings.'*
Creating Places, Northern Ireland Planning Service (2000)

Foreword

An important part of our role is to raise standards and set new quality, design and sustainability benchmarks for the industry. We put the needs and priorities of the people who live and work in the communities we serve at the heart of our work.

So much so that we've published a consultation on future housing design and sustainability to stimulate debate on how we should prioritise the quality of new housing in a challenging financial climate.

By testing new ways of working, promoting innovative approaches, adopting challenging standards and championing skills and knowledge, we support our partners to create and maintain thriving communities.

Our portfolio of resources, best practice examples and training programmes supports the industry to ensure we deliver quality affordable homes; employment and skills opportunities for local people; and communities with good transport links, local amenities and green spaces.

We've created a new tool for planners, councillors and developers that helps assess the design quality of planning and development applications. Qualityreviewer can help set a project brief, steer communications and discussions about a scheme and assess the scheme as the design evolves.

This guide will help all those involved in the planning and development process to raise the design standards of a range of schemes from historic and rural developments to coastal and urban projects.

Qualityreviewer will play a valuable role in helping to create thriving places that will stand the test of time.

Sir Bob Kerslake
Chief Executive
Homes and Communities Agency

Planning for quality

Every year local authorities determine hundreds of thousands of planning applications. The proposed developments range from household extensions to new settlements. Each one is an opportunity to achieve social, economic and environmental benefits, and to contribute to making a successful and sustainable place. Each of these decisions will have an impact on how resources are used.

Local authority members and officers can make a difference. They influence the use, design and form of buildings and spaces through their vision of what places can become, through their leadership, and through insisting on quality.

The best planning is based on sound policy and effective management of the development process. The aim of development management is not just to make decisions on planning applications, but to help people to build the right development in the right places. Qualityreviewer is part of a new, positive approach to development management, focusing on quality right at the start of the process.

Until the 1990s the planning system in the UK was concerned with land use (deciding which uses should go in which location), and very little with the physical form of buildings and spaces, apart from highway layouts. Achieving high standards of design was largely left to good clients and talented designers.

But the physical form of development plays an important part in determining if a place is successful, and if national priorities (such as tackling climate change and promoting inclusive design) are achieved. This realisation has led to aspects of design being brought under planning control over the past decade. The

Kings Place, at London's Kings Cross, is an office building and arts venue designed by Jeremy Dixon and Ed Jones. Its triple-layered, west-facing glass screen has a practical function of protecting against the heat and glare of the sun. Its wave-like form, shimmering in the changing light, is also strikingly beautiful.

planning system now seeks to influence a development's layout, its height, its massing, and its appearance. It seeks not just to manage land use, but to support the creation of successful places and respond to the challenge of climate change.

Making places should be a democratic process. The people who live and work in a place should be involved in deciding what it should become. Design involves choices. At its best the planning system can ensure that the right choices are made, by the right people. Qualityreviewer is a means of helping to achieve that.

Many people in central and local government, and in government agencies and the built environment professions, are committed to raising standards of design. CABE, Architecture and Design Scotland, the Design Commission for Wales and others provide valuable guidance, and effective enabling and design review services.

But more than three quarters of planning applications are prepared by someone with no design training. For the foreseeable future the system's commitment to quality will be largely in the hands of planners, councillors and other decision-makers who have little or no design training. Many of them are passionate about the qualities of the places where they live and work, and they tend to learn about design from experience.

Qualityreviewer has been created to help them think about the design and quality of development when they manage development. It will also be helpful to many other people who play a part in determining the quality of places, whether or not they are trained or experienced in design. Even when their decisions seem not to be of great significance, the cumulative effect of those decisions on the quality of life and on our impact on the planet may be immense.

Qualityreviewer breaks down the question 'Will this planning proposal produce a well-designed development?' into a series of steps. These steps do not themselves answer the question. Design is not like that. Instead Qualityreviewer helps people appraising development proposals to reach a balanced decision after thinking systematically.

UNDERSTANDING CHARACTER

Qualityreviewer reflects an awareness that in current planning practice too often a superficial assessment of 'character' distorts a local authority's consideration of design quality (see pages 61–8). More fundamental – and often less subjective – attributes of a development proposal are overshadowed.

Understanding the distinctive character of a place is essential in designing for that place or appraising a development proposal. But character is not something separate from a place's other attributes: it is made up of them. Qualityreviewer gets to grips with these essentials.

How to use Qualityreviewer

Qualityreviewer is a guide to thinking about design quality. It can be used as a step-by-step guide to appraising development proposals, large and small, or in structuring other planning processes or documents. Its aim is to help local authorities and others become more effective in achieving planning's local, regional and national objectives. A large number of policy and guidance documents already set out these objectives for a wide range of contexts. Qualityreviewer helps to achieve them.

Qualityreviewer is no substitute for having the right skills or getting the necessary expert help. Indeed, when used alongside the skills audit method Capacitycheck, it can help local authorities identify what they need to do to bridge any skills gap.

'Qualityreviewer at glance' (page 30) can be scanned or photocopied to record the conclusions (in outline in the case of a more complex proposal) of pre-application discussions; a design statement; or a design appraisal.

The diagram below shows how to use Qualityreviewer in appraising development proposals. A fuller version of the diagram, setting out the method's wider applications, is on page 100.

USING QUALITYREVIEWER TO APPRAISE DEVELOPMENT PROPOSALS

Who uses Qualityreviewer	Stage in the planning process	How Qualityreviewer can help
Client/developer, design team and local authority	**Pre-application discussions**	The client and design team discuss initial appraisals, design principles and proposals with the local authority, using Qualityreviewer to set design priorities. They identify the need for any further specific appraisals (see pages 12–23)
Design team	**Design and access statement**	The design team prepares a design statement (for submission with the planning application), setting it out using the Qualityreviewer structure (see page 97). A concise design statement will often be useful even if it is not formally required
Consultees	**Consultees' appraisal**	Consultees consider the planning application using the questions in Qualityreviewer at a glance (see pages 30–1)
Local authority	**Local authority's appraisal**	The local authority appraises the application using Qualityreviewer (see page 28)
Local authority	**Planning decision**	The planning committee or (if the decision has been delegated) the planning officer considers the application in the light of the Qualityreviewer appraisal (see page 29)

A major development on what was a large gap site in a south coast town forms a new street frontage. An attempt has been made to create a prominent feature at the point of pedestrian access through the block.

Part A
Qualityreviewer method

Understand the place

1 Site and context appraisal

2 How policy and guidance apply

Understand the proposal

3 Concept

4 Impact

5 Design quality

6 Team

Understand the implementation

7 Execution

8 Management and maintenance

Make the decision

9 Information and advice

10 A balanced decision

Understand the place
1 Site and context appraisal

We can design a successful scheme or appraise a planning proposal only if we have a good understanding of the place: not just the development site but also the wider area. Listed below are topics that we may have to focus on to understand the site and its context. Which of the topics are relevant or important will depend on the circumstances and on the nature of the development proposal. Building for Life (see page 103) also provides useful guidance on analysing a site and its context.

Understanding places and appraising them are not purely technical matters. Many judgements depend on the perspectives and values of the people who are making them. Those who carry out any place appraisal that is not wholly subjective will want to consult the people who live, work or otherwise have a stake in the area. They may use a participatory appraisal method such as Placecheck (a simple method of appraising any place) or Spaceshaper (CABE Space's method of appraising public space).

One of the most important aspects of the appraisal will be to understand the potential of the place to contribute to tackling climate change. Many historic places that developed in a low-carbon society and economy retain characteristics that favour creating low-carbon development today. The best design will make the most of those characteristics, and of the potential to make good use of buildings and structures that already exist.

Every site is different. It is never appropriate blindly to copy a design that seems to have been successful in another location. Understanding the place is the key to good design.

DIAGRAMS

The essentials of the scheme's context can be shown by drawing some simple diagrams. You might draw the diagrams if you are a planner analysing a proposal, or a designer explaining the proposal in a design and access statement; or you might look at them if you are a councillor or member of a design panel who has requested them, to understand the site better.

Several characteristics of the existing site can be combined on a single diagram if appropriate, or several diagrams may be drawn to illustrate a single issue. The diagrams can be simple sketches on tracing paper or on the site plans themselves, often needing only a couple of different pen or marker colours.

Knowing how a place developed helps us understand how a variety of buildings can create a harmonious whole.

TOPICS FOR CONTEXT APPRAISAL

Form and setting

- Natural setting and ecology
- Historical, cultural, social and economic context
- Buildings, spaces and structures
- Materials
- Greenspace
- Movement and inclusive access
- Public transport
- Parking
- Land ownership
- Management and maintenance

The uninterrupted building line of this London street holds it together visually despite the varied size of its buildings.

People

- Emotional needs (how does the place effect people's emotions?)
- Sensory experience (what do people sense?)
- Factors contributing to health (what influences health here?)
- Safety and security (what issues relating to personal safety and security of property are important here?)
- Equality and inclusiveness (what aspects need to be taken into account?)

Servicing
(location, capacity and expansion capability)

- Water
- Energy
- Telecommunications
- Waste
- Utilities

A new house on the Hebridean island of Gigha, where until 2002 only one new house had been built in the past 30 years. Community ownership of the island gave Gigha a new chance after decades of stagnation, and locally appropriate forms of development had to be designed.

Understand the place
2 How policy and guidance apply

The local authorities that are most effective in supporting high standards of design have well-conceived policy and guidance that expresses their vision for the place. In preparing to appraise the development proposal, we need to establish:

Blank walls create dead streets.

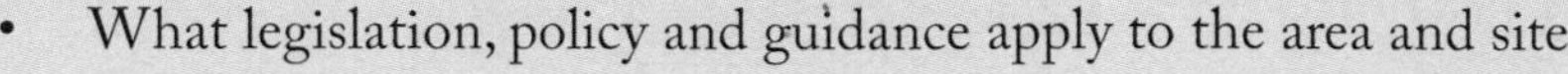

- What legislation, policy and guidance apply to the area and site.

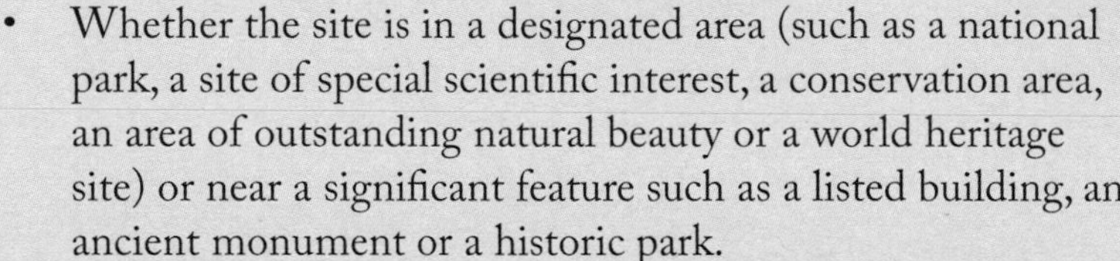

- Whether the site is in a designated area (such as a national park, a site of special scientific interest, a conservation area, an area of outstanding natural beauty or a world heritage site) or near a significant feature such as a listed building, an ancient monument or a historic park.

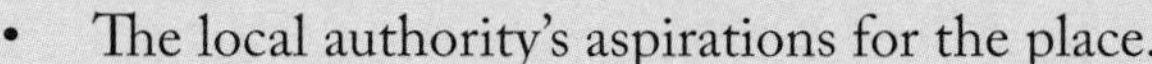

- The local authority's aspirations for the place.

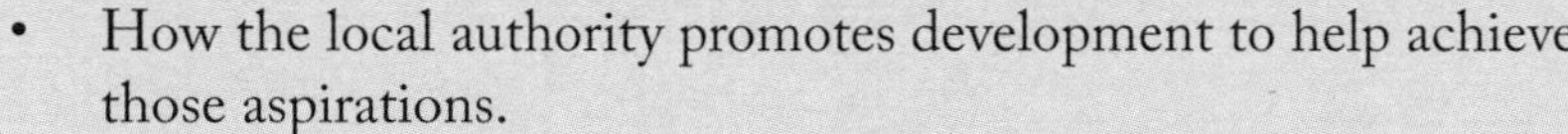

- How the local authority promotes development to help achieve those aspirations.

Every local planning authority must produce a local development framework. At the heart of this is the core strategy, a document describing the local authority's vision for its area over the next 15-20 years. The core strategy must explain how the place works, what its strengths and weaknesses are, and what makes it special. On the basis of this understanding, the core strategy will state the local authority's aspirations for the area (conceived with full public involvement) and explain how these will be achieved. The strategy will reflect national policy priorities, such as those for tackling climate change and the need for design to be inclusive.

A series of related development plan documents or supplementary planning documents will provide more detail. Together, the documents that make up the local development framework provide the local authority's policy and guidance on planning and design. This specifies and explains how development can contribute to creating successful places in the local authority's area. It will provide a firm basis for appraising the design quality of development proposals.

The local authority will be effective in raising standards of planning and design if its work is based on a full understanding of the area's life and characteristics, and if it has put a clear and realistic vision at the heart of the planning process.

National policy and guidance will include (where applicable) planning policy statements and guidance by government and other organisations (such as the CLG/CABE *By Design* and the Homes and Communities Agency's two-volume *Urban Design Compendium*). The table on page 21 shows how these documents relate to each other.

Access to this west London hotel seems to have been designed with cars, not pedestrians, in mind.

Regional policy and guidance includes regional spatial strategies. Local development frameworks will be complemented by local guidance: area action plans, design guides, urban design frameworks, masterplans, design codes, development briefs and conservation area character appraisals. The best local policy and guidance will be based on creative thinking, on the involvement of local residents and other stakeholders, and on a realistic understanding of what can be delivered.

Policy, guidance and regulations should be judged critically. Some of it will have to be followed, and will give weight to the planning decision. Other policy, guidance and regulations, even if it is not mandatory, may be based on sound thinking and will contribute to making a sound decision. But some policy, guidance and regulations may be irrelevant to the particular case or out of date. It is important to identify which is which.

Consider which of the following are up to date and relevant to the development proposal, and whether they relate to placemaking:

- Policy and guidance at regional and local levels.
- Policy and guidance at national and European levels.
- Legislation, policy, guidance, regulations, duties, standards and precedence that need to be complied with.
- Legislation, policy, guidance, regulations, duties, standards and precedence that should be considered but do not necessarily need to be complied with. (The distinctions are important. Regulations that have significant impacts on places are often applied unthinkingly as though they were mandatory, instead of thoughtful consideration being given to what the place needs.)

The coffee shop at the front of this south London supermarket helps to bring the street to life.

ROBUST DECISIONS

The importance of expressing any planning decision in terms of policy and guidance can be seen when decisions are challenged at planning appeals. When planning inspectors support the local authority's decision, they usually note how the local authority's decision has been grounded in carefully considered design guidance (based on a sound understanding of the context); how that guidance was based on well-conceived local policy (expressing the local authority's vision of what qualities it aspires to create for the place); and how both the guidance and the policy were drawn up with full public consultation, and in the light of national policy and guidance.

Qualityreviewer helps local authorities to meet the call in *Planning Policy Statement 1 (PPS1): Delivering Sustainable Development* for a considered, comprehensive and consistent approach to design policies, based on understanding the local area. PPS1 states that design is not a subjective issue: 'decisions about it should be based on a clear policy framework with design principles and criteria agreed by both professionals and communities'.

Understand the proposal
3 Concept

First, we need to understand the project's concept. What is the development proposal intended to achieve, and how? What are its essentials? How does the proposal relate to a vision for the wider area beyond the development site?

If the planning application is accompanied by a design statement (see page 96), or a draft proposal by a draft statement, this should specify (as required by government regulations): the amount of development; the layout; the scale; the landscaping; the vehicular and transport links; and the inclusive access. This information should convey the essentials of the proposal.

ASPIRATIONS

Second, we need to understand the project's aspirations and precedents. What local examples set a standard worth emulating? Has the project been inspired by celebrated examples from wider afield? The examples need not necessarily be for the same use. A wide range of publications, websites and study tours is available to point the way. Identifying such benchmarks can be helpful in appraising the development proposal.

A design may be unique to its context, but most developments follow a basic pattern. The planning applicant should be able to point to successful precedents. For example, if the development is a shopping centre in a town centre, the applicant should be able to show successful examples of a similar approach. It will be important to agree what is meant by success.

If there are no examples of a similar design working successfully elsewhere, it may be either because this is the result of a brilliantly innovative creative leap, or because the designer has failed to learn from experience and best practice. It is important to find out which it is.

Innovation in design is valuable when it represents imaginative thinking about how to respond to a complex brief and a rich context, but not when it results from little more than a desire to be different and to attract notice.

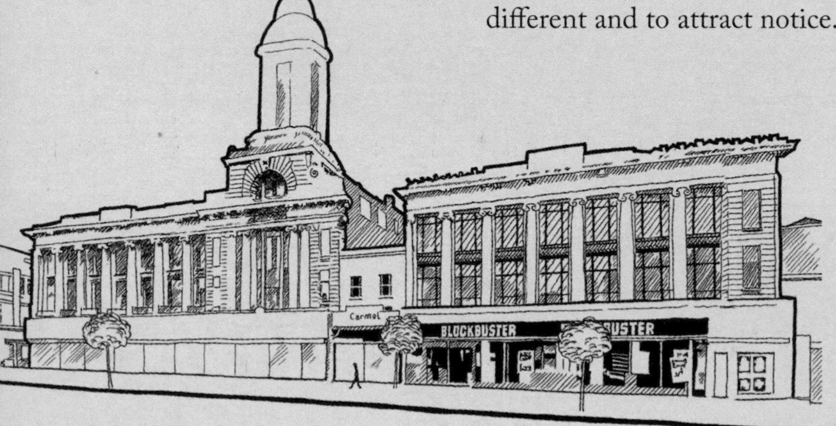

One shop owner in this street in Whitechapel, east London, refused to sell up, but the developer of the department store was confident that he would give in eventually. How wrong he was!

EXAMPLE: A NEW BUILDING THAT DID NOT LOOK OLD

An enforcement appeal concerned a farmhouse and related complex of barns on the edge of Newcastle-upon-Tyne. After nine unsuccessful planning applications, the buildings had been converted and added to, without planning permission, in a manner that the appellant claimed was an appropriate character and appearance.

The inspector disagreed. 'The development has been built using modern construction techniques and the external walls are constructed in blockwork with stone facing,' he wrote. 'Unlike on a converted stone barn, the stonework shows no signs of bulging or subsidence and has a new appearance. Furthermore, there are typical signs of modern construction such as vertical movement joints, segmented flat stone lintels that are almost certainly supported by hidden steel lintels, and regular window head heights.'

The inspector continued: 'In addition, roof planes are flat and ridges are horizontal without any sagging. The development as a whole has a new-build appearance and does not have the inherent character of a converted collection of redundant agricultural buildings. The development has a new-build character and appearance in a countryside setting and has harmed the visual amenity of the green belt.' The inspector dismissed the appeal and upheld the enforcement notice.

The suggestion that new construction next to a historic building should itself give the impression of being old is a strange concept. Whatever its style, a new building should not have to pretend to be anything but new. If the design of a proposed new building is not good enough to complement its historic neighbour, it should not receive planning permission.

EXAMPLE: A MISSED OPPORTUNITY TO CREATE A PUBLIC SPACE

This housing development on the edge of a village in Scotland has a green space. Some of the houses front on to it. Having buildings fronting on to public space normally works well. But some of the houses back on to the open space, presenting their garden fences to it. This is likely to be more of a security hazard than if the gardens backed on to other gardens. Having the backs of buildings backing on to open space tends to make the space feel dead. There seems to be no reason why this space could not have been fronted by houses on all sides.

The development's roads make no contribution to the area's traffic circulation, except for accommodating that generated by the houses themselves. Its roads do not provide through routes to anywhere. There are plans to develop the adjoining field in a similar way. This new development will also be connected to the highway network at a single point. It will have no connection by road or footpath to the development shown here.

This process may continue as further fields are developed. The village as a whole will grow ever bigger but only as a series of parts, none connected to any of the others. None of the parts will be designed in a way that will encourage people to walk. None will help to create a street with enough footfall or car traffic to support local shops or other uses. A clear concept is needed.

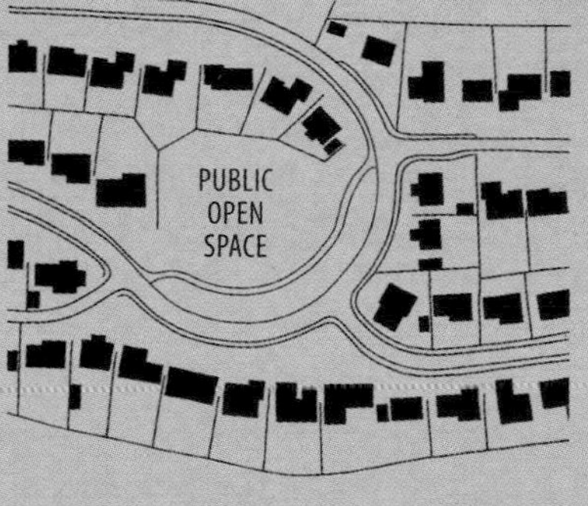

A plan of the housing scheme's open space; and a view of the side of the space that is fronted by houses (the other side is fronted by the back fences of gardens). See also the diagram on page 37.

In the shadow of St Paul's Cathedral in London, the redevelopment of Paternoster Square had a major impact on a much-loved setting. Many schemes were designed and abandoned before this one was finally built.

Understand the proposal
4 Impact

Consider how significant the impact of this development proposal is likely to be, and the influence of this on how the development proposal will be handled.

The likely impact will depend on two things: first, the significance of the site and, second, the nature of the proposal. Any policy and guidance that relates specifically to the site should itself reflect an understanding of its significance.

Is development on this site likely to have an important social, economic, environmental or cultural impact? Will that impact be only local, or will it be felt more widely? Which particular groups of people will be affected more than others? Answering these questions will be a step towards understanding the place, and will later help in conceiving or appraising a specific development proposal.

The likely impact of the development proposal will determine what resources the local authority (or other public agency) will devote to ensuring a high standard of planning and design; what processes (such as consultation) will be required; what appraisals will be carried out; what negotiations will take place; which team of officers will be involved; and how they will work together. The more important the development, the more attention and the more rigorous analysis it will merit.

Think about the impact in terms of the following aspects of development:

- Size (how large is the proposed development?)
- Historic context (how sensitive is its historic context?)
- Townscape and landscape (what impact will it have on the appearance of the place?)
- Visibility (what impact will it have on views?)
- Social impact (what impact will it have on its neighbours, the community and people further afield?)
- Environmental and ecological impact (including impact on the use of non-renewable resources, and impact on carbon emissions and local climate change)
- Economic impact
- Favourable or detrimental impact to other places

The local authority took enforcement action against this UPVC first-floor bay window extension, and the homeowner's appeal was dismissed. The planning inspector recognised that the design of the neighbouring houses and their architectural features did not 'exhibit a coherent theme', but found the bay window 'incongruous', 'out of character with the surrounding development', 'overbearing' and 'discordant'.

This is planning at its smallest scale. Deciding such cases will depend on appraising the impact of the development itself, and of the cumulative impact of many such developments.

In each case it may be important to ask: What type of impact? What severity? Impact on whom? Even if the impact is minor when considered on a city-wide scale, it may be significant at the scale of a neighbourhood or for local residents.

And even if the impact of the development itself is not significant, the impact of many such developments may well be. Often the gradual improvement or decline of a place is the result of innumerable small changes, each of which may have seemed unimportant at the time. Consider whether the development proposal will set a precedent for a positive or negative cumulative impact.

A number of other impacts may also need to be considered through formal assessments as part of the planning process. For example, environmental impact assessment is a procedure that must be followed for certain types of development before they are granted planning permission. The procedure requires the developer to compile an environmental statement, describing the likely significant effects of the development on the environment, and proposing mitigation measures. Where a new development is likely to have significant transport implications, a transport assessment should be prepared and submitted with the planning application.

There are likely to be specific triggers to requirements for various assessments – the number of houses in a development, for example. But significance is more subtle than that: a 10-unit housing development in one location may be more significant than a 100-unit development in another.

In using Qualityreviewer, it may be appropriate to grade the impact of the proposed development (on the range of users or groups) as very significant; fairly significant; or of minimal significance, understanding the positive and negative impacts of each.

Understand the proposal
5 Design quality

Traditionally, the treatment of a building's facades would often reflect the importance of the streets that they fronted.

Consider what the proposed development's strengths and weaknesses are in relation to the six sets of design qualities (which are discussed more fully in Part B, pages 34–91):

- Movement and legibility
- Space and enclosure
- Mixed uses and tenures
- Adaptability and resilience
- Resources and efficiency
- Architecture and townscape

MOVEMENT AND LEGIBILITY

- Does the design give priority to easy access for pedestrians (of all abilities)?
- Will the development encourage the use of public transport?
- Will the development be well connected to important destinations and routes?
- Who will the development make welcome and comfortable?

Imaginative design turned a brief for a public convenience and flower stall in a dead space in west London into a delightful green-tiled building with a large public clock.

SPACE AND ENCLOSURE

- Will the development reinforce the street's building line or erode it?
- To what extent will the development help to frame and enclose streets and public spaces?

MIXED USES AND TENURES

- What will the development do to promote mixed uses and tenures at the appropriate level (building, block, neighbourhood or district)?

ADAPTABILITY AND RESILIENCE

- How could the development be adapted to a new use or uses if conditions change?
- Will the development contribute to tackling climate change, and to adapting to and mitigating its effects?

Jubilee Library in Brighton succeeds in being relatively efficient in its use of energy. Air is cooled by being passed through the precast hollow-core concrete slabs that form the floors and ceiling, rather than by more energy-intensive means. On warm days fresh air is drawn into the main library hall and exhausted through the rooftop wind towers.

RESOURCES AND EFFICIENCY

- Will the development use resources efficiently in construction and operation?

ARCHITECTURE AND TOWNSCAPE

- How successfully will the development be integrated into its setting?
- How functional will the development be?
- How attractive will the development be?

GUIDANCE ON DESIGN QUALITY

Most design policy and guidance for planning in the UK is broadly related to themes that Qualityreviewer focuses on: movement and legibility; space and enclosure; mixed uses and tenures; adaptability and resilience; resources and efficiency; and architecture and townscape. Local authorities write their own policy and guidance in the context of the relevant national framework. There is some variation in the precise terms used. The table shows how these themes are covered in six of the UK's most important guidance documents on design.

Two aspects of Qualityreviewer will be particularly helpful in relation to policy and guidance. First (as discussed on pages 61–8), the planning system often deals with design in a way that puts excessive emphasis on character. Qualityreviewer tackles this by focusing on the attributes of a place that actually shape its character, rather than seeing character as being something separate.

Second, Qualityreviewer reflects current concerns about design and the use of resources in the light of climate change, in a way that some earlier design guidance (such as *By Design*, published in 2000) does not.

Qualityreviewer	Movement and legibility	Space and enclosure	Mixed uses and tenures	Adaptability and resilience	Resources and efficiency	Architecture and townscape
Urban Design Compendium (England, 2001)	Make connections	Places for people Work with the landscape	Mix uses and form	Design for change	Manage the investment	Enrich the existing
By Design (England, 2000)	Ease of movement Legibility	Continuity and enclosure Quality of the public realm	Diversity	Adaptability		Character
Designing Places (Scotland, 2001)	Ease of movement A sense of welcome	Safe and pleasant spaces		Adaptability	Manage the investment	Identity
A Model Design Guide for Wales Residential Development (Wales, 2005)	Accessibility and ease of movement Legibility	Continuity and enclosure Public realm	Variety and diversity	Adaptability	Resource efficiency Compactness	Natural heritage Character and context
Technical Advice Note 12: Design (Wales, revised 2009)	Ease of access for all Legible development	Successful relationship between public and private space High quality in the public realm	Quality, choice and variety		Sustainable design solutions	Character Innovative design
Creating Places: achieving quality in residential developments (Northern Ireland, 2000)	Ease of movement	Security and vitality			Quality and sustainability	Sense of place Visually attractive human scale Appropriate planting

Understand the proposal
6 Team

Find out if the proposal has been designed by a person or team with design training and with a track record of good design. If members of the team are young and untested, make sure that their work receives the scrutiny it needs.

A large proportion of planning applications are prepared by someone without formal design training, including plan drawers, property agents, builders and computer-aided-design technicians. Of those who have been trained in design, some are used to designing in one specific context, but may have little skill in designing in an urban, suburban or rural context.

If the design is being (or has been) developed by a team, it is important to find out if the team has (or had) the right skills for the job. Capacitycheck (the urban design skills appraisal method that is a companion method to Qualityreviewer) may be helpful in this.

It may be useful to review how successful the individual's – or team's – previous work has been. Lack of success may not necessarily be a reason not to use that designer or team: the problem might have been the client, the brief, the political context or the budget. And designers at the start of their careers need to be given their chances. In these circumstances it is especially important for the planning process to be used to help achieve design quality.

What attributes the designer or design team needs will depend on the nature of the project. Consider which of these are relevant, and ask the developer to provide the information:

ATTRIBUTES OF A DESIGNER OR DESIGN TEAM

- Skills
- Qualifications
- Awards
- Experience
- Creativity
- Design approach
- Client recommendations
- Membership of approved practitioners lists (such as development agencies' design panels)

Understanding the designer or design team and their track record can guide the local authority in its discussions with the applicant, and its decisions about what time and resources to allocate to the planning application.

Whatever the qualities of the designer or design team, these will be made full use of only if the designers are fully engaged with the appropriate authorities and stakeholders throughout the process.

If the design team is not adequate for the job, the consultations with the local authority (and more widely) may lead the developer to augment the team with additional members and skills, or to take a different design approach.

In the case of a major development, the local authority will need to be sure that its own team is up to the job of making the most of this development proposal, from pre-application discussions to application appraisal.

EXAMPLE: A JUSTIFIABLY INWARD-LOOKING BUILDING

Here the design team – the celebrated Swedish-based architect Ralph Erskine working with British architects – recognised that it is sometimes appropriate for a building to turn in on itself. The site of the Ark in Hammersmith, west London, is bounded by major roads (including the Hammersmith flyover, seen here) and railway lines. The Ark does not ignore its surroundings: it is a landmark designed to be seen from passing vehicles.

The copper-clad building was built in 1992. The original concept was of an internal street as the focus for the office accommodation. With terraces, bridges, hanging gardens and pergolas, it was an inspiring building. It was never commercially successful, though, and recently new owners brought in a new team to redesign the interior.

The Ark: designed for hostile surroundings.

EXAMPLE: A BUILDING TO BE NOTICED

The architect Zaha Hadid designed an extension to an Oxford college (our drawing is based on the architect's computer-generated image). The extension is to a Victorian building in a Victorian suburb.

Clients do not commission Hadid (architect of the London Olympics aquatic centre) in the hope of getting a building that will not be noticed. The proposed extension does not look like a conventional building at all. If it were not designed by a world-famous architect, such a design would be very unlikely to get planning permission. If it is built, it will no doubt become celebrated as a rare example of the work of an architect who has built very little in the UK. The quality of such a building will depend on the beauty of its sculpted forms and its internal spaces, the ingenuity of how it accommodates its functions and the exquisiteness of its detailing.

Zaha Hadid's Oxford proposal.

Understand the implementation
7 Execution

Consider whether the design is likely to be well executed.

Many developments that initially look promising, later turn out to suffer from poor detailing or construction, or they are not built to the agreed design. To avoid this, planning authorities should follow these guidance points:

A permanent sign warns of a characteristic of the British Library's piazza that its designers did not expect.

- Outline applications
  Ensure that outline planning applications (see page 98) are handled in a way that specifies design principles and the quality of design from the start.

- Detailed applications
  Use planning conditions to ensure that the design, detailing and construction will be of high quality.

- Minor (or non-material) amendments
  Be careful in considering minor amendments that will erode design quality.

- Phasing
  Ensure that the phasing of the stages of development has been planned in a way that will deliver the development's most important features.

Too often the budget for a development scheme's landscape works is cut at a late stage in the project, and what was promised is never achieved. At Birmingham's Brindleyplace, by contrast, the landscape works were completed – and even the fountains were working – before the buildings were constructed. The message was clear: this is a place where quality matters.

- Legal agreements
  Use legal agreements to protect design quality where appropriate. These may include planning gain agreements; covenants to ensure effective maintenance; legal agreements allowing a former landowner to retain the power to approve the design of development schemes; restrictions by landlords on certain design or alteration work by tenants; and arrangements by which a landlord, local authority or housing association hands over title to a site only when the development has been satisfactorily completed.

- Outcome review
  Review the outcomes of planning decisions so that any loss of design quality can be identified and procedures can be improved.

- Enforcement
  Use enforcement powers to remedy failures to build to the required standard, creating a reputation for strict enforcement.

The piers of this wall were to have been topped with carefully designed copings, but they ended up with paving slabs.

Developers may themselves suggest suitable conditions or legal agreements (often setting them out in the design statement). They can also review the outcomes of the development process to help in raising their own design standards.

See CABE's document *Protecting Design Quality in Planning* for further guidance on this. Building for Life (see page 103) can also be useful in considering whether the design is likely to be well executed.

EXAMPLE: FAILURE TO SUSTAIN A CULTURAL COMMITMENT

The British Film Institute's London IMAX Cinema was built in 1999, with Lottery funding. Being sited on what had been a public space (which was later occupied by homeless people in what became known as 'cardboard city'), the windowless building was locally controversial. Local people were promised that each year a vast artwork would be commissioned for the cinema's rotunda. The first was a mural by the distinguished British artist Howard Hodgkin.

To the anger of local residents, the idea of displaying artworks has since been abandoned in favour of commercial advertising for such products as mobile phones and (seen here) chocolate bars. In urging the local authority to take enforcement action, the local MP wrote: 'The IMAX is itself demeaned as a cultural building by the replacement of artworks by commercial advertising, and the site is surrounded by listed buildings. I would be extremely concerned if instead of being a visible gateway to the South Bank cultural quarter, the IMAX sacrificed its arts identity to become just a commercial hoarding.'

London's IMAX cinema: a cultural landmark advertising chocolate bars.

The timber cladding and porch of a new small house. How long the timber lasts will depend on what it is, how it has been detailed and how it will be maintained.

Understand the implementation
8 Management and maintenance

Consider whether the development is likely to be well managed and maintained after construction.

Even if the development is well designed and well built, these efforts will be wasted if it is not well managed and well maintained. Generally a building or space will begin to deteriorate as soon as it is completed unless satisfactory arrangements are made to look after it. In many cases it may be difficult to find out much about management and maintenance, but it is important to think about what to ask.

MANAGEMENT AND MAINTENANCE: WHAT TO ASK

- Is it clear who owns what, and who will be responsible for management and maintenance?
- Are the management and maintenance likely to be effective?
- Have issues of financial viability (on which successful management and maintenance depend) been carefully considered?
- Will the type of tenure affect how the development will be managed and maintained?
- Will the design of the development make it easy to manage and maintain to a high standard?
- Will the materials be robust, and easy to maintain or replace?
- Will long-term maintenance provide employment for local skilled trades and crafts people?
- Will the development provide adequately for storage and recycling, and for the storage and collection of waste?

Courtyards in the Crown Street regeneration area (see page 44) provide private and shared green space. Maintenance and servicing arrangements were thought out early in the design process.

Make the decision
9 Information and advice

The previous steps may have highlighted matters on which more information is needed before the development proposal can be fully appraised. If so, ask the planning applicant for the necessary information.

Government advice reminds local authorities only to ask for information that is relevant, necessary, proportionate, and justified by national and local policy.

GETTING HELP

Local authorities will need help with at least some aspects of improving and appraising the design of planning proposals. Some of the necessary skills may already be available among local authority staff: Capacitycheck can help to identify them.

In the longer term existing staff can be trained in design; new staff with the necessary skills can be recruited; specialist staff can be shared with other local authorities; consultants can be hired; other agencies, such as English Heritage or a regional architecture and built environment centre may provide design advice or support; and in some cases additional local authority staff can be paid for by (but not answerable to) major developers. CABE is setting up a nationwide network of accredited Building for Life assessors to help local authorities and government organisations assess the design quality of new housing developments.

Qualityreviewer can be used for all types and scales of development. There are several other appraisal methods and services that can be valuable in particular cases. These include:

- ATLAS
- BREEAM and other environmental assessments
- Building for Life
- Code for Sustainable Homes
- Design Quality Indicator
- Design review
- Secured by Design

See Appendix 1 (page 103) for more details of these methods.

This house in Milton Keynes has been carefully designed around an internal courtyard. To the street it offers blank walls. Does the setting of this building justify the blank facades, or should windows and doors have been provided to bring some life to the street, and to create a sense of the street being overlooked?

Make the decision
10 A balanced decision

Some aspects of development are considered to be so important that government initiatives are devoted to them. These include design, inclusive design, climate change, sustainability, social cohesion, economic development, crime and community safety. None of these is an absolute that must be considered in isolation of the others. The job of appraising planning applications always involves understanding how all of these matters can be balanced in the way that is appropriate to the circumstances.

In appraising a planning proposal, a local authority will consider whether this will be a successful development on its own terms. For example, if it is a shop, is it likely to attract customers (including those with access difficulties) and to be convenient for deliveries? If a house, will it be a pleasant and convenient place to live?

The local authority will appraise whether the development is likely to be valued in the long term. This may not be the first concern of whoever is commissioning it if their main objective is to sell it and move on, but it will be a prime concern of the local authority.

The appraising of the planning application will consider how much thinking has gone into the design, and what the quality of that thinking was. Much poor design is a result of thoughtlessness: working in a hurry, applying standard solutions or using standard products. Some poor design follows a significant amount of thinking, but the thinking is based on inadequate skills, an inappropriate design approach, a bad brief, an inadequate budget (for design or construction), or inadequate understanding of (or concern for) the context.

The Agricultural Business Centre in Bakewell houses a livestock market, Business Link, farmers' market and public rooms. In the Peak District National Park it was important to have a carefully designed building such as this, not an industrial shed.

An appraisal needs to be based on an understanding of what values (and whose values) the design is based on. A successful design balances the potentially conflicting perspectives of different groups of people: old and young people, people with differing degrees of mobility, people travelling on foot or by car, building users and passers-by, and so on. The aim of the development management process is to make a balanced decision in the public interest, mediated through the planning system.

How easy it is to appraise a development or a development proposal depends on what there is to appraise. Appraising the quality of a completed building is relatively easy. Appraising the likely quality of a planning proposal on the basis of limited information is a great deal more difficult.

Ease of appraising design quality	
Easier ↑	A development that has stood the test of time
	A development built a few years ago
	A newly completed development
	A planning proposal presented at design review with a relatively high quality of graphic and in-person presentations
	A planning proposal that is well-presented and accompanied by a good design statement
More difficult ↓	A planning proposal that is poorly presented and lacks a useful design statement

THE APPRAISAL DECISION

Planning Policy Statement 1: Delivering Sustainable Development, which sets out the government's planning policies for England, states: 'Design which is inappropriate in its context, or which fails to take the opportunities available for improving the character and quality of an area and the way it functions, should not be accepted.'

When you have understood the place, understood the proposal and appraised it (calling on expert help where necessary), ask:

- Is the development proposal good enough to be granted planning permission?
- Does the proposal raise issues that will be the basis for a) grounds for negotiation; b) conditions on a planning approval; or c) reasons for refusal?

Decide whether the development proposal should be:
- Accepted
- Accepted with conditions
- Negotiated, or
- Rejected

Qualityreviewer at a glance

Use this form (download it from www.qualityreviewer.co.uk) to highlight the findings of a fuller analysis.

Scheme reference: ______________________

Tick which applies:

☐ For pre-application discussions ☐ For a design and access statement ☐ For appraising a proposal

Understand the place

1 Site and context appraisal (see page 12)
What is special about the place?

2 How policy and guidance applies (see page 14)
How should policy and guidance be applied?

Understand the proposal

3 Concept (see page 16)
What is the design concept?

4 Impact (see page 18)
How significant is the scheme's impact likely to be?

5 Design quality (see page 20 and Part B, page 33)
What are the design's strengths and weaknesses?

• Movement and legibility	
• Space and enclosure	
• Mixed uses and tenures	
• Adaptability and resilience	

• Resources and efficiency	
• Architecture and townscape	

6 Team (see page 22)
Does the design team have the right skills and approach?

Understand the implementation

7 Execution (see page 24)
How can we ensure that the design will be well executed?

8 Management and maintenance (see page 26)
Is the scheme likely to be well managed and maintained?

Make the decision

9 Information and advice (see page 27)
Do we need more information and advice?

10 A balanced decision (see page 28)

• For pre-application discussions: are there any outstanding issues?	
• For a design and access statement: is the statement complete and satisfactory?	
• For appraisal: a. is the design good enough?	
b. should the proposal be accepted/ accepted with conditions/ negotiated/or rejected?	

The cluster was chosen as the preferred development pattern for the Hebridean island of Gigha, when in 2002 community ownership of the island at last made development possible. Based on the form of a traditional Gigha farm steading, a cluster allows small buildings to be extended at a later date. This can provide more living or working accommodation, car parking, a garage, a workshop or storage space. Gigha's clusters avoid inappropriate streets and cul-de-sacs without leading to unacceptably fragmented development. They are energy-efficient, with buildings usually orientated to minimise exposure to prevailing winds and to maximise exposure to the sun.

Part B
Thinking about design quality

Using diagrams

Six sets of design qualities

- Movement and legibility
- Space and enclosure
- Mixed uses and tenures
- Adaptability and resilience
- Resources and efficiency
- Architecture and townscape

Using diagrams

Drawing simple diagrams can help us to understand a development proposal in the context of the site and wider area. The diagrams may reveal aspects of the design that would create difficulties if changes were not made. Too often such basic problems are overlooked, while more superficial defects become the main points of discussion or disagreement between the applicant and the local authority.

The applicant, knowing that this sort of information is what the planners are likely to be looking for, may decide to include these diagrams in any design statement. This can be very helpful. If such diagrams are provided, those appraising the scheme may want to check on the quality and accuracy of each of them.

The diagrams shown here are examples, not a comprehensive list of all the diagrams that might be useful in various circumstances. Usually a diagram should show the context, not just the site. Here the surroundings have been omitted for the sake of simplicity.

WHAT THE DIAGRAM SHOWS	WHY IT MATTERS	WHICH ATTRIBUTES OF DEVELOPMENT THIS RELATES TO MOST CLOSELY	WHAT SORT OF DIAGRAMS TO DRAW
Concept and layout: landscape and built form	The basic forms of landscape, street blocks, plots and buildings are the starting point for successful design	Movement and legibility Adaptability and resilience Resources and efficiency	Plan showing main elements of landscape and built form; section through the site and area
Micro-climate	The micro-climate is a major influence on the use of non-renewable resources and on personal comfort	Space and enclosure Adaptability and resilience Resources and efficiency Architecture and townscape	Diagram showing north point, sun path, prevailing wind, and shelter elements
Movement: pedestrian and vehicular routes	How people get around and how the development is connected into the surrounding area are major influences on how the place works and what it feels like	Movement and legibility Space and enclosure Adaptability and resilience	Diagram of main and secondary vehicular routes, and pedestrian and public transport routes
Uses, tenures and densities	The mixes of uses, tenures and densities help to determine the activities in the area, and how diverse and adaptable the place is	Movement and legibility Mixed uses and tenures Adaptability and resilience Resources and efficiency	Diagrams showing ground- and upper-storey uses, tenure mix and densities
Views	Views in and out of a place help to determine how attractive it is and how easily people can find their way around	Movement and legibility Space and enclosure	Diagram showing views to and from proposed buildings and space

WHAT THESE DIAGRAMS HELP YOU TO THINK ABOUT	EXAMPLE OF DIAGRAM
Does the design pay due regard to the site's most significant features? Does it respond effectively to the public interest and the client's brief?	Concept (Crown Street regeneration area, see page 44) — Central spine and neighbourhood heart - - Neighbourhood links 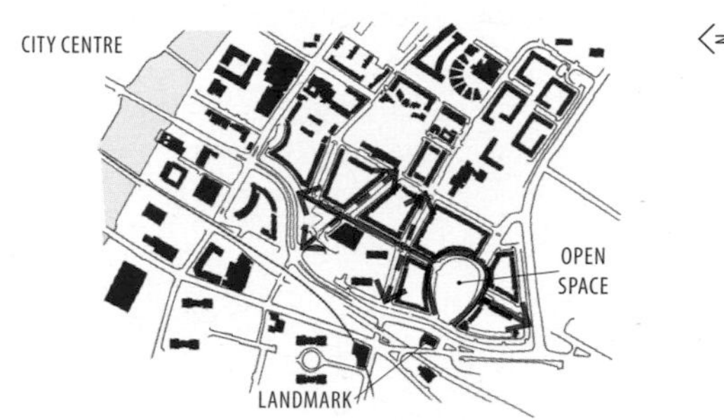
Does the design minimise carbon emissions and the use of non-renewable resources, and maximise comfort in the environment?	Microclimate (the BO 01 waterfront development, Malmo, Sweden) → Prevailing winds — Tall buildings as wind break - - Staggered streets prevent wind tunnelling □ Sheltered public space 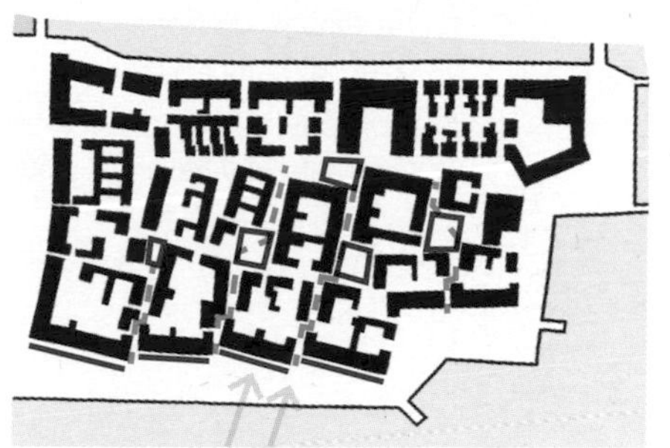
Does the design give priority to easy access for pedestrians (of all abilities)? Will the development encourage the use of public transport? Will the development be well connected to important destinations and routes?	Movement (Accordia, Cambridge, see page 88) — Primary street - - Secondary street → Entrance → Pedestrian and cycle access 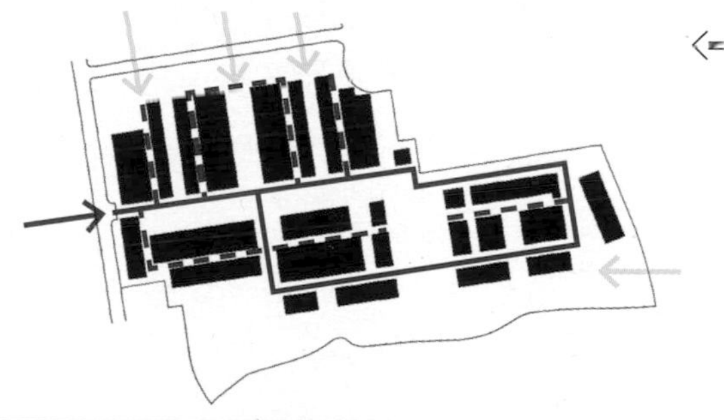
Will the development contribute to creating an appropriate mix of uses, tenures and densities in the area?	Proposed ground floor uses (Laurieston, Glasgow) School Commercial Residential Existing buildings Existing street blocks outside the masterplan area 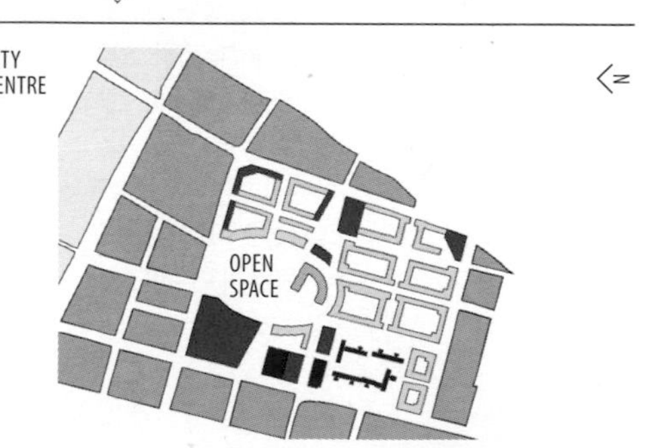
Does the design make the most of potential views?	Views (Gun Wharf, Plymouth, see page 50) — Views 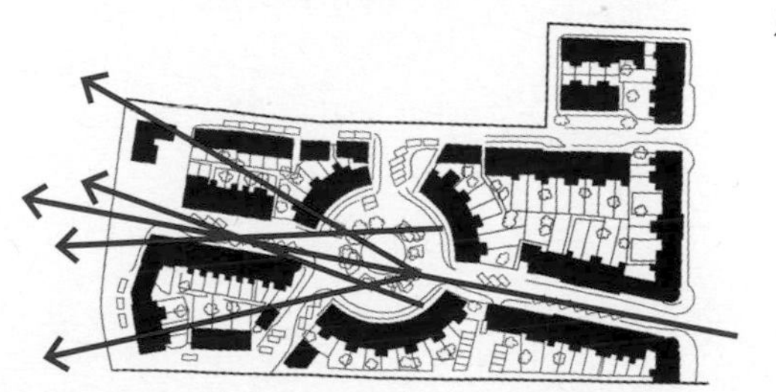

WHAT THE DIAGRAM SHOWS	WHY IT MATTERS	WHICH ATTRIBUTES OF DEVELOPMENT THIS RELATES TO MOST CLOSELY	WHAT SORT OF DIAGRAMS TO DRAW	WHAT THESE DIAGRAMS HELP YOU TO THINK ABOUT
Building lines along the street	How buildings line the street helps to determine how the place works, how it feels and the sense of enclosure	Movement and legibility Space and enclosure Architecture and townscape	Diagram with lines showing where and how buildings meet the street	Does the design relate well to the line of other buildings along the street?
Building heights, roofline, skyline and massing	The configuration of buildings influences the quality of the views, townscape and the sense of enclosure of space	Movement and legibility Space and enclosure Architecture and townscape	Diagram with lines (plan and elevation)	Does the design create a successful roofline? Is the scale of the building appropriate? Which parts of the site will be in shadow?
Public space, private space and ambiguous space	In successful places public and private space is generally clearly distinguished. Ambiguous space is often troublesome	Movement and legibility Space and enclosure Adaptability and resilience	Diagram with shading	Does the design clearly distinguish public and private space (actual and perceived)?
Front doors	Front doors indicate buildings' public faces. The relationship of building fronts to public space is often a key to successful design	Movement and legibility Space and enclosure Architecture and townscape	Diagram with arrows	Does the design make front doors relate well to public space?
Live frontage: active (or mainly active) walls	Blank walls create dead spaces	Space and enclosure Architecture and townscape	Diagram with lines	Does the design create live frontages where approriate?

EXAMPLE OF DIAGRAM

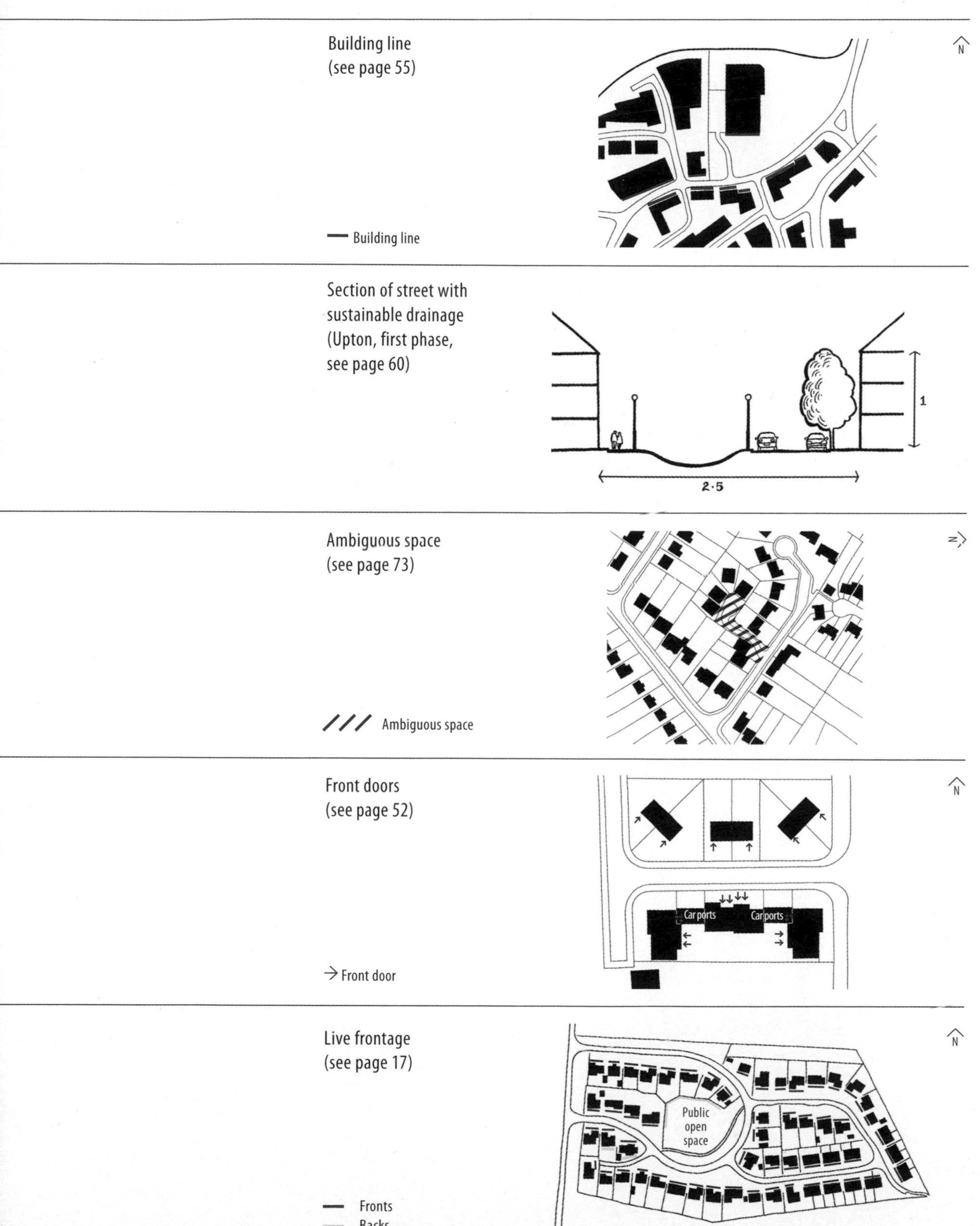

Six sets of design qualities

Qualityreviewer focuses on the proposed development's strengths and weaknesses in relation to six sets of design qualities:

- Movement and legibility
- Space and enclosure
- Mixed uses and tenures
- Adaptability and resilience
- Resources and efficiency
- Architecture and townscape

Part B explains these concepts, and suggests how to use them in thinking about design quality.

Movement and legibility

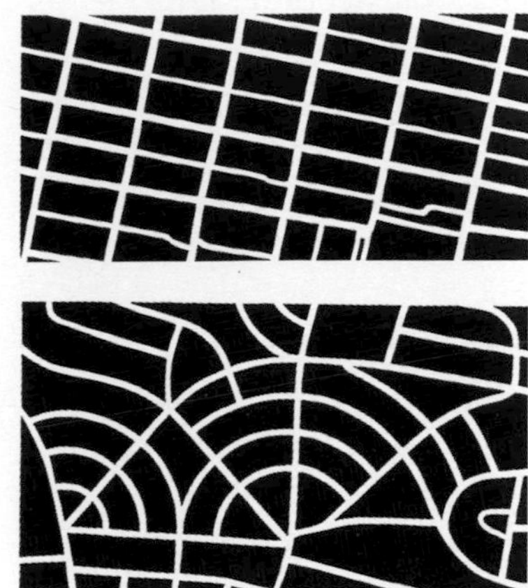

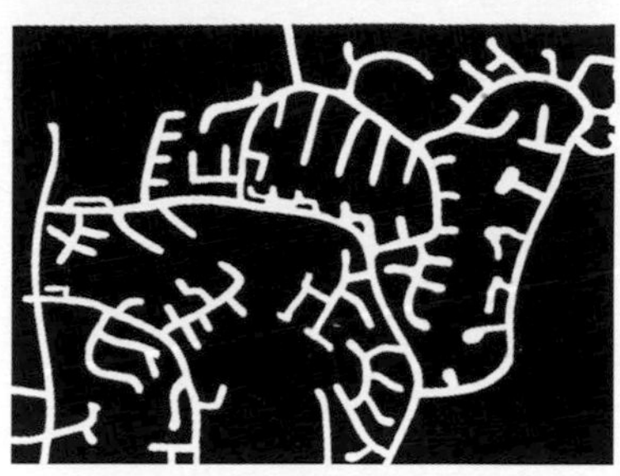

Three distinctive street patterns in Glasgow: the 18th and 19th century city centre (top); a 1950s suburban council estate (middle); and 1980s suburban cul-de-sacs (bottom).

Designers love creating pictures, full of happy people, of places they have designed and hope to see built. Whether or not the place will be full of people in reality depends not just on how well the buildings and the spaces have been designed, but on how well the place has been connected into every kind of route.

Every development of any significant size has an impact on how easily people can move around on foot, by wheelchair, with walking aids, with a buggy, by car, by public transport or by any other means. The layout of any development will largely determine the patterns of movement. Those patterns will in turn influence the character of the area; how welcoming it feels; how adaptable it is; how pleasant its public spaces are; and what mix of uses can be sustained.

We can tell a great deal about a place from a simple representation of its layout, such as a figure-ground diagram (in which buildings are shown in black, and public places in white) or the pages of an A-Z guide. It is usually possible to tell by looking at a page of the A-Z of any town or city a fair amount about what the development in a particular location will be like.

The intricate network of streets and alleys is likely to be the town's medieval core. The tight grid will usually be Victorian or Edwardian terraces or urban blocks. The varied geometric layout is likely to be inter-war semi-detached or detached houses, or a 1950s council estate. The strangely shaped blocks set at right angles to each other, but without apparent streets, will be 1960s or 70s council estates. The wriggly worm shapes will be 1970s, 80s or 90s cul-de-sacs. In each case we will be able to make an educated guess at what the place would be like to visit.

Urban designers call for places to be 'legible' – easy for people to understand and find their way around. Generally a feature of anything well designed – whether it be as small as a household utensil or as large as a new urban quarter – is that it is easy to sense how it works. Not only can someone visiting the place for the first time find their way around easily, but strangers feel at ease and sense they have a right to be there.

Historic places have a different kind of legibility. It may be easy to get lost in a maze of historic streets and alleys, but the life and diversity of the place can make the experience a delightful one. The place reveals its story in subtle ways.

INCLUSIVE DESIGN

Design should be inclusive. The philosophy of 'inclusive design' is evolving, rather than being a fixed set of design criteria. The aim of creating an inclusive environment is not to meet every need, but to remove barriers and features leading to exclusion and to maximise access for everyone. It is important not to segregate access and facilities for disabled people or see them as add-ons, but to ensure that full access is integrated into all design features.

An inclusive environment will be used easily by as many people as possible without undue effort, special treatment or separation. It will offer people the freedom to choose how they access and use it, and to participate equally in all activities that take place there. It accommodates diversity and difference, and it is safe, legible, predictable and logical. The aim should be to give everyone as much choice as possible in moving around on foot, wheelchair, bike, or with a buggy, and not having to rely on a car or some other means of transport. Design should ensure that there are no hazards or obstructions for people with sensory impairments.

There may be difficult conflicts to resolve, particularly where people and vehicles mix. The needs of wheelchair users and people with walking difficulties, on the one hand, may conflict with those of people with sight difficulties, on the other. A kerb may be a hazard or barrier for one group while for others it may be a potentially useful physical guide.

The first thing we need to know about a building is where the entrance is. The doorways of this Georgian house (now a doctor's surgery, left) and the modern office building (above), both in London, are their facades' primary decorative features. Little else is needed.

EXAMPLE: AN ATTEMPT TO MAKE REAL RESIDENTIAL STREETS

The grounds of a former mental hospital at Charlton Down, a few miles from Dorchester in Dorset, have been developed for housing, having been classified as a brownfield site. The site is poorly connected to its surroundings, but the local authority, the developer and the architects have given a great deal more thought to the design than most housing developments enjoy.

The aim was to create streets that had something of the character of a traditional village, rather than a suburban housing estate. This has been achieved by siting houses at the edge of the pavement, building walls between them to maintain the building line, and providing some of the parking in garages hidden behind the timber gates in those walls. Unfortunately opening the gates seems sometimes to be too much effort and many of the residents seem to prefer to park on the pavements. More rigorous parking enforcement might be a solution to that.

Other parking is provided in the middle of the street blocks in what are both living and parking courts. It is difficult to create something that is not a street, but that provides parking, access to garages, and is fronted by houses. Here the asphalted spaces lack the attractiveness of Charlton Down's actual streets and create a less legible network of pedestrian alleys.

Case Study
A new neighbourhood with connected streets

South of Glasgow city centre, the Crown Street regeneration area occupies the site of a failed 1960s council housing scheme. That housing had replaced Europe's most notorious slums, the Gorbals. The success of Crown Street as a neighbourhood with mixed uses and a range of facilities has led to the masterplanning and redevelopment of two adjacent areas.

The Crown Street masterplan has created a network of connected tree-lined streets, faced with mainly four-storey buildings, inspired by Glasgow's traditional tenements. Within the street blocks are green areas, providing residents with private and semi-private space. The clear distinction between private and public space makes maintenance responsibilities clear.

Representatives of the community council were involved throughout the decision-making process. The use of design competitions has kept standards high.

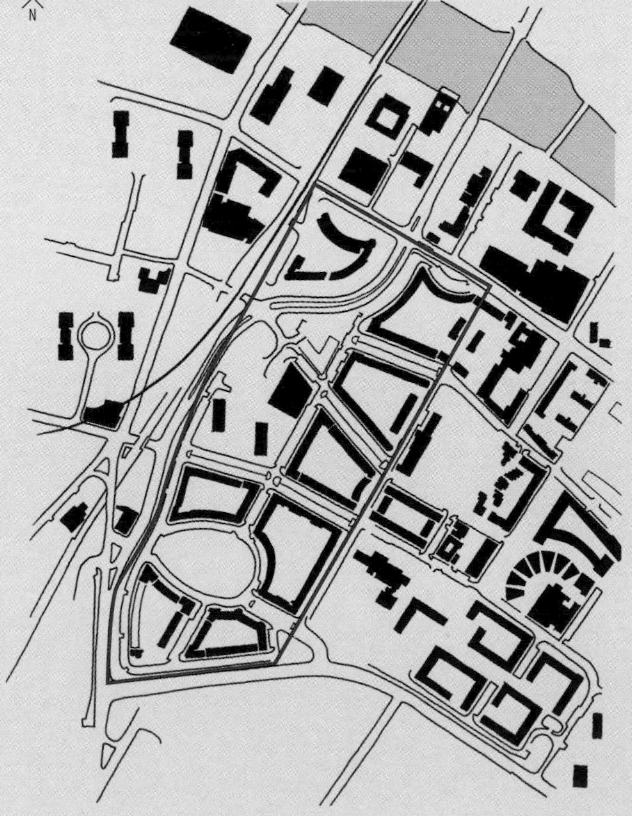

The street on the north side of the Crown Street regeneration area's public park frames a ruined church by the great Victorian architect Alexander 'Greek' Thomson (right). The dramatic roof of this apartment block (far left, below) provides a focal point to Crown Street itself. Parking is provided in the centre of the area's broad streets (left). The new local centre (below) provides a small supermarket, a library and several smaller shops.

Space and enclosure

Whoever is paying for a development will have their own objectives. They may plan to sell or rent it, or use it to accommodate their business or their family. They may have no particular concern for the people for whom the building provides part of the backdrop to their lives.

But those wider interests certainly should be concerns of the local authority. The council will ask what any development will do to make the public realm (places that are available for everyone to see, use, enjoy, and have free and legal access at any time, including streets, squares and parks) more pleasant, more adaptable, more welcoming and easier to move around.

Think of a built space you love. The chances are that it is enclosed by buildings that look out on to it. Then think about the sort of place that could be anywhere and is almost everywhere. Some buildings turn their backs to the street. Others are set back from the street behind space for parked cars. There is little sense of enclosure, creating a poor relationship between the building and public spaces.

Urban buildings that follow a continuous building line around a street block often contribute more to making a successful place than individual buildings located in the middle of a large site. Buildings with active edges (such as shopfronts, doors opening on to the street, or residential upper floors) enable people to keep an eye on public space and make it feel safer. Clearly defining and enclosing private space at the back of buildings, whether for amenity or servicing purposes, tends to create better privacy and security.

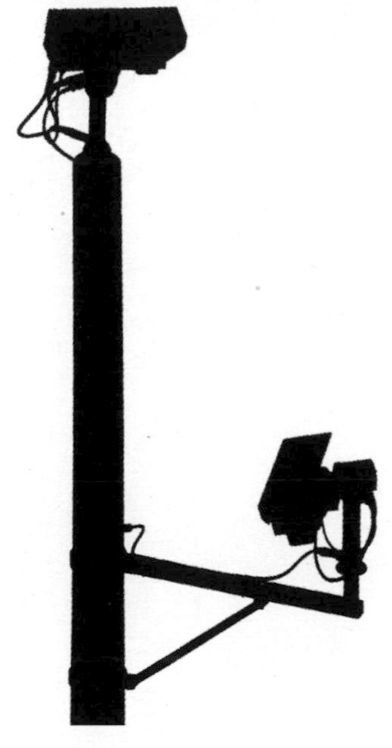

There are often more friendly means of making a place feel safe than resorting to the technology of closed-circuit television.

Successful streets and other public spaces channel movement and concentrate activity, with a clear relationship between frontages and public space.

Selfridges at Birmingham's Bullring shopping centre can justifiably be claimed as an architectural icon, passing the test of being featured on picture postcards. But the long rear elevation (above) does nothing at all for the liveliness or interest of the street.

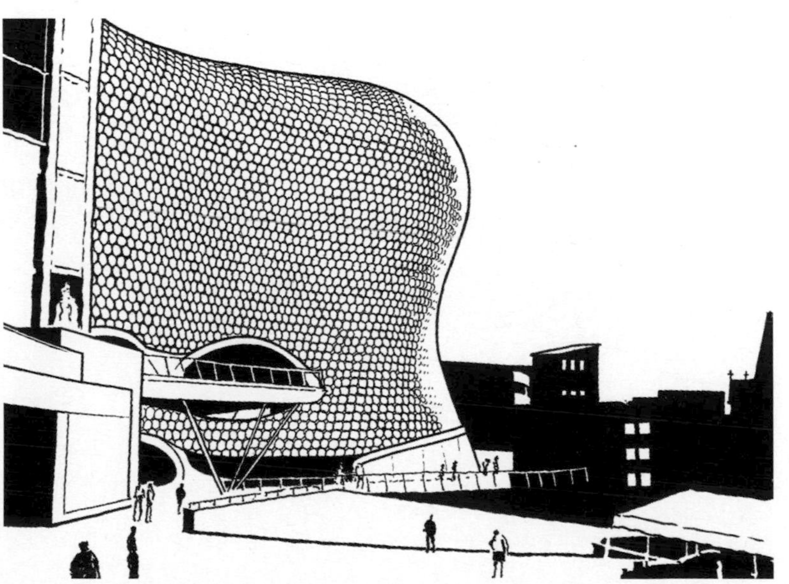

SPACE AND ENCLOSURE: WHAT TO ASK

Building line

- Will the development reinforce the street's building line or erode it?

Continuity and enclosure

- To what extent will the development help to frame and enclose streets and public spaces?

Public and private space

- How well will the development help to define public spaces (such as streets, squares and parks) and private spaces (such as gardens and yards)?

Left-over space

- Will there be any spaces lacking a clear function, and lacking anyone with a sense of ownership and responsibility for maintenance?

No aspect of housing design needs more thought than the question of what happens between the front of the building and the street. Here the space is used for parking, but very little thought seems to have been given to its design.

Private space

- To what extent will private gardens, yards and balconies be provided?
- How secure will these spaces be?

Streets

- What kind of environment will the streets present?
- Will they be well landscaped?
- Will cars dominate streets?
- Will pedestrians feel safe and comfortable using them?
- Will there be a range of street types?
- Will the proportions be pleasing and comfortable?

Public spaces

- What public spaces will be created or improved?
- Will they feel safe?
- Will they be well overlooked?
- Will they be located at centres of activity or other places that will encourage movement through them?

Activity

- How will the proposal help to create active streets and spaces (by front doors opening on to the street and windows overlooking the street, for example)?
- Will shops and businesses front the streets and spaces?

New development in an east London street maintains the building line and roof line.

Providing additional parking in the courtyard could have allowed active uses at the ground floor, helping to create a more inviting space.

Case study
Shared space and street life

Gun Wharf in Plymouth is something rare: a new residential area that has a character of its own, that makes strangers feel that they have a right to be there, and that seems to encourage residents to come out on to the street and chat. Far from being a lucky accident, this has been achieved by thoughtful design.

The existing buildings have been carefully knitted into the new development; the streets are connected, rather than creating one or more dead ends (despite the site being constrained on two sides by the historic dockyard wall and on the third by the waterfront); the steep slope has been used cleverly to make the most of the views over the estuary and to provide varied means of access for people with limited mobility; and the parking has been successfully integrated into the street scene (there is only one parking court at Gun Wharf).

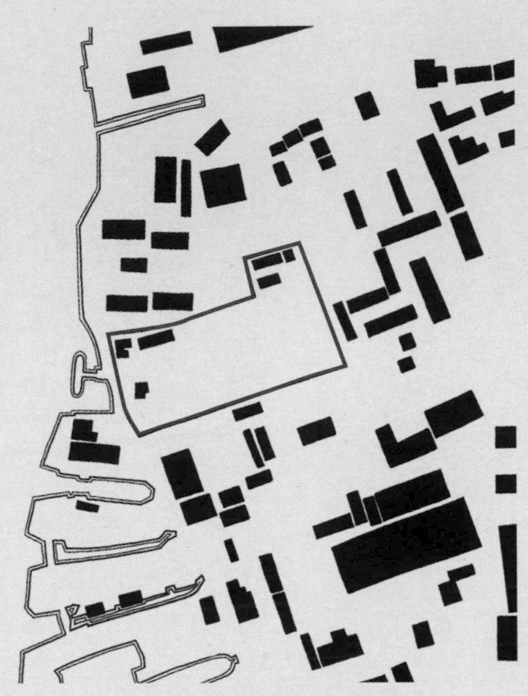

A context plan (top) and a plan showing the clear distinction between shared and private space at Gun Wharf.

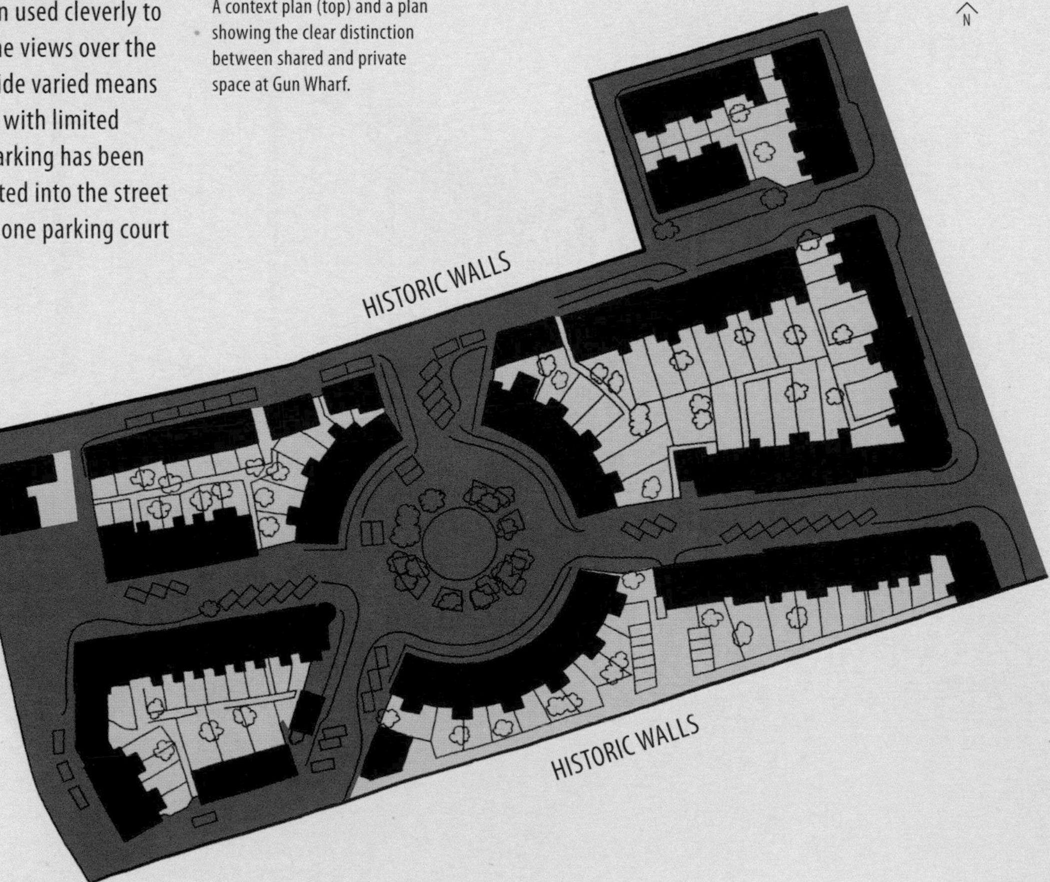

Gun Wharf is a designated home zone, where pedestrians and cyclists have priority over cars.

The circular open space at Gun Wharf is a good example of inclusive design. There is access by steps with handrails, and well-designed slopes lead to level spaces. Popular as a children's play area, it is more versatile than traditional grassed spaces.

The sloping site at Gun Wharf poses a number of challenges for less able people, but a positive approach to inclusive design has helped to mitigate some of them. Access from the sloping street to the houses has been helped by providing landings with steps at one end and gentle ramps at the other, working with the site's topography.

Case study
An ambiguous relationship with the street

Three pairs of rundown, semi detached council houses have been demolished in the suburbs of a northern city, leaving a sloping site on which a housing association has built 12 apartments. The doors to half the apartments face the street. The other half are around the back. To reach them, residents or visitors go through to the back of the triple carports, making their way between the cars. These doors lead to a shared garden to which some of the apartments have direct access. Some of the ground floor apartments have patio doors that open on to this semi-communal space.

Whether the residents feel confident enough to leave those patio doors open in fine weather will depend on how far they trust their neighbours and how they assess the risk of untrustworthy people coming through to the back. Those same matters will affect how safe and communal the shared garden feels.

The other housing in the area consists of semi-detached council houses whose front doors lead through front gardens to front gates to the street. The new housing departs from this pattern. Its long side presents the street with the triple carports and the asphalt which leads to them. The other two sides do not present any doors to the street. At the east end there are not even any windows at the ground floor level, only a blank brick wall: the ground floor of the flats has been raised up to take account of the site's slope.

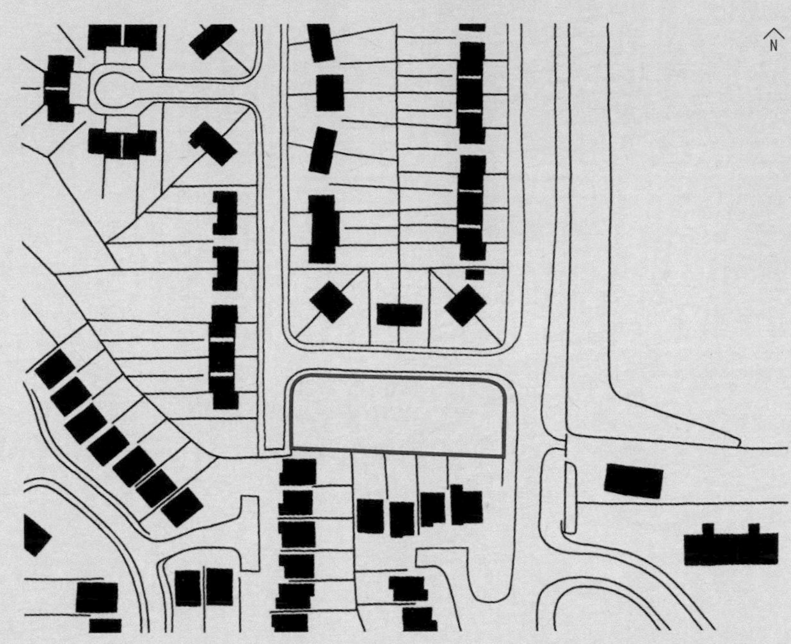

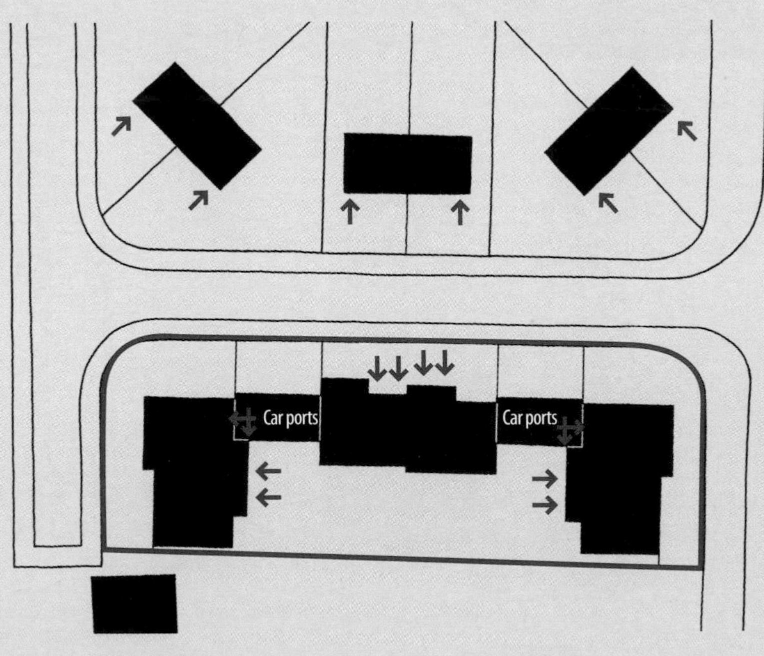

A context plan (top); and a plan showing the locations of front doors.

Neither end of the development (top) presents any doors to the street. The communal space (middle) provides access to some of the apartments' front doors. Some of the front doors, and the doors leading to some of the other apartments, are awkwardly located at the back of the car ports (left).

Mixed uses and tenures

It is often easiest to build a place with just one use: a retail park, a business park, a leisure park, a shopping centre, a housing development and so on. The best-loved places are rarely like that.

Successful places tend to have a lot going on. People are there for different purposes, and they do not know whom they will meet. If any one of the place's activities becomes no longer viable, there will be others to continue bringing it to life. Often different activities will be happening at various times of the day and night.

The mixed uses and tenures that support diversity can be provided within an individual building by stacking different uses or tenures on different floors, or by locating different uses and tenures next to each other or within a wider area. The local authority should ask of any development: what will it do to promote mixed uses and tenures at whatever level is appropriate (building, block, neighbourhood or district)?

Knowing how a mix of uses can contribute to making a successful place, planners sometimes insist on them even in places where they will not be supported, perhaps colouring an area of a plan as being for mixed uses. That is often pointless. Whether a particular street will support mixed uses will depend on, among other things, how it is connected to other streets and to the local pattern of movement. It is no good specifying a street as being for a mix of commercial and other uses if there are unlikely to be enough people passing along it to make any commercial use viable.

This development in London's docklands provides a mix of private, shared-ownership and social-rented homes.

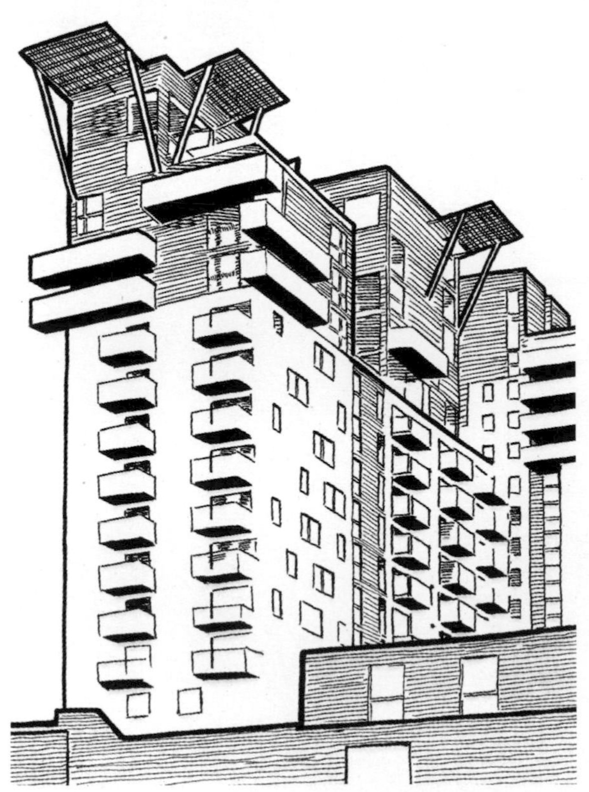

MIXED USES AND TENURES: WHAT TO ASK

- Will public spaces allow for a variety of uses?
- Will the infrastructure (including water supply, sewerage, drainage, gas, electricity, cable, telephone, roads, footpaths and cycleways) be adaptable and easily accessible to accommodate future uses?
- Will the scheme be designed for a range of uses to change in time?
- Will the scheme be able to accommodate a mix of tenures?
- Will the mix of uses and tenures offer choice to people of different ages and levels of income?

Case study
Not just a big box in a car park

A superstore operator applied for planning permission for this site at the edge of the town centre, overlooking the estuary on the south coast of England. The planning department was happy with the amount of shopping and parking, but dismayed by the proposal: a big-box store in a sea of car parking. The planners persuaded the superstore to think again, and to hire urban designers. The result was a new proposal. The store was moved to the front of the site, with the side facing the street being lined with small shop units and accommodating an entrance to the store. Apartments would be built above the shops. Some of the parking would be provided in an upper deck, freeing up part of the site for other uses: housing, offices, a hotel and a waterside walkway.

As built, the scheme largely follows the form of the revised plan. The major differences are that the small shop units lining the street were never built, nor is there an entrance to the superstore from the street. Instead the street is faced by dull window displays, with no view from the street into the store. Perhaps the superstore operators did not want competition from small shop units, preferring that any shopping be done in the store itself.

Even the local authority's urban designers doubted whether there would be adequate footfall to sustain small shops in that location. In such circumstances it would make sense to design the building so that it could be adapted to accommodate small shops facing the street at a later date, if patterns of development and pedestrian flows change in a way that will support that kind of retail use.

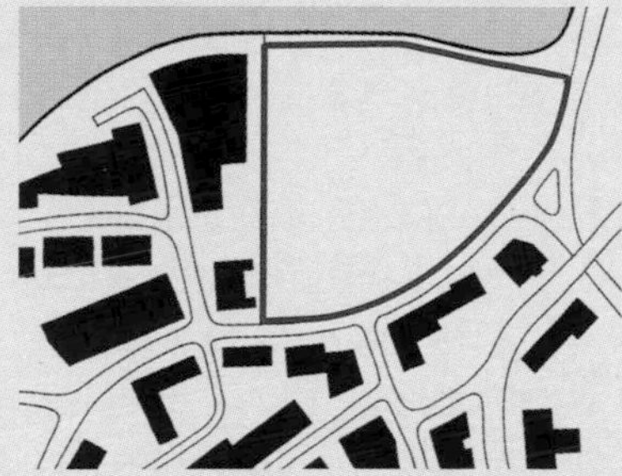

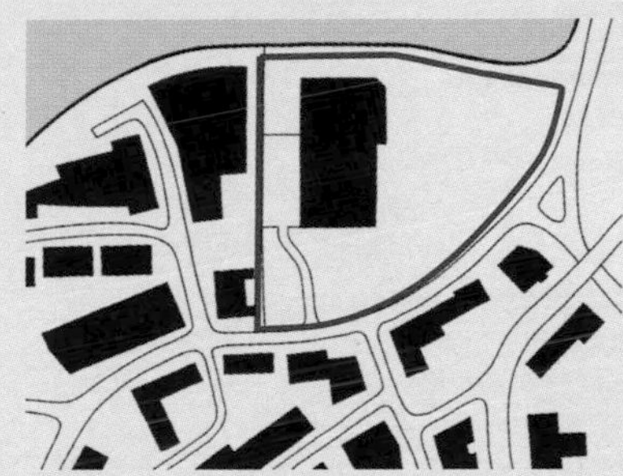

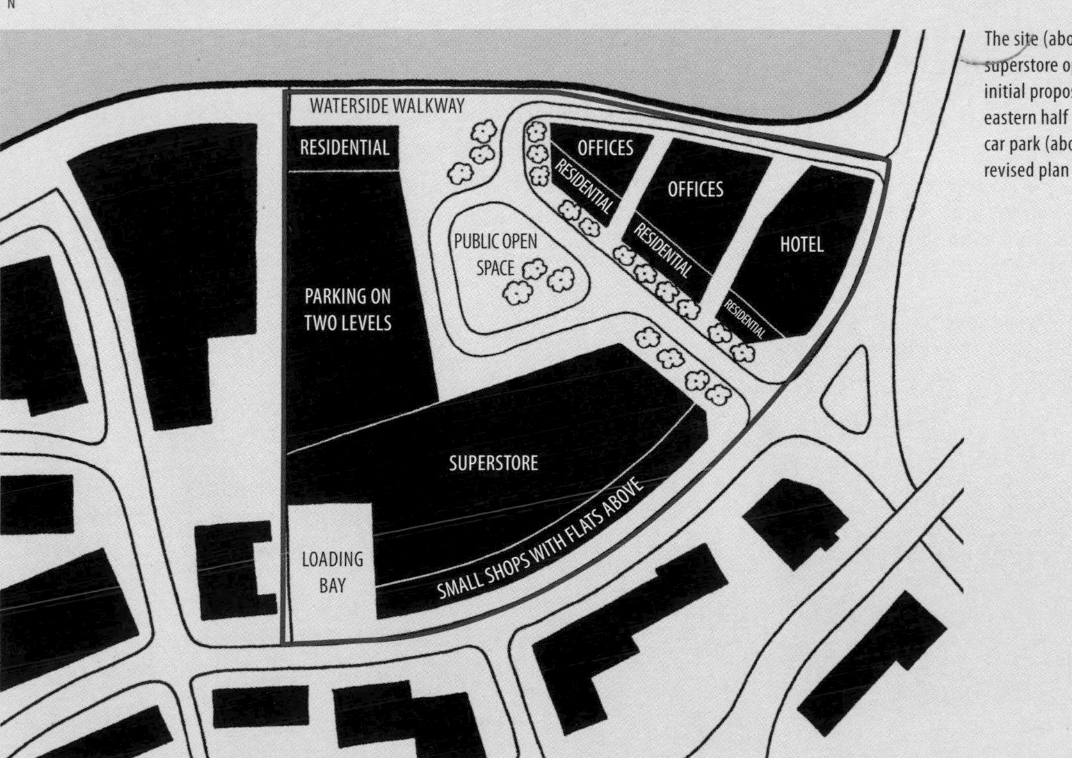

The site (above left); the superstore operator's initial proposal, with the eastern half of the site as car park (above); and the revised plan (left).

The houses in a conservation area in Waterloo, London, have adapted to changing ways of living over a period of 170 years.

Finch Lane in the City of London has existed since at least the thirteenth century, although all its buildings are later. Buildings may come and go, but we can expect street layouts to survive.

The developer of these three houses near Cardiff has claimed a degree of adaptability: the ground floor and parking areas could be converted to liveable rooms, with the parking moving on to the street.

This house in a mews at Accordia in Cambridge (see page 88) has a flexible ground-floor space for parking and other uses.

Adaptability and resilience

The one thing we know about any place is that it will change. We do not know much about how people will live, work, shop and use their leisure time in 10, 20 or 30 years time. We certainly do not know how the climate will change. Places change unpredictably in response to social, economic, environmental and technical changes about which planners may have little more idea than anyone else.

Successful places flourish under differing conditions by being adaptable. Their buildings may change from houses, to shops, to offices, and back again. They do not all have to change at the same time. The structure of the building may make it adaptable.

For example, if a new community does not initially have enough inhabitants to support shops, some houses may be built with floor-to-ceiling heights that make them suitable for conversion to shops later. In other cases the adaptability may derive from the layout of the streets. Connected streets are more likely to be adaptable than cul-de-sacs, which attract no one who does not live there.

A local authority should ask of any development: how could it be adapted to a new use if conditions change? In an extreme case, if the development is a nuclear power station, for example, we know that the development will have only one use. But we should ask how the infrastructure might be re-used after the power station has been decommissioned.

In any historic town the streets are likely to be much older than the buildings. The streets' adaptability will have contributed to making the place successful, and is likely to continue to do so. Modern street patterns may also last a long time if they are well designed. If they prove not to be adaptable, on the other hand, the process of change is likely to be unnecessarily painful, expensive and wasteful.

ADAPTABILITY AND RESILIENCE: WHAT TO ASK

- Will the development contribute to tackling climate change, and to adapting to and mitigating its effects?
- How adaptable is the infrastructure layout? Will it be able to accommodate alternative uses and buildings in the future?
- How could the development be adapted to a new use or uses if conditions change?

BedZED (Beddington Zero Energy Development) in south London, with 82 homes, is one of the best-known pioneers of energy-efficient housing. Many more such experiments are needed to develop new ways of urban living.

Resources and efficiency

At a time when facing up to climate change should have the highest priority, the efficient use of resources is an essential element of design quality. Every development should contribute to tackling climate change, and adapting to and mitigating its effects.

The proposed development's use of resources should be considered specifically. But it should also be considered as a major element of the other attributes of places (movement and legibility, space and enclosure, mixed uses and tenures, adaptability and resilience, and architecture and townscape). Each attribute will help to shape the place's social, economic, environmental and cultural life for a long time. There is nothing so wasteful of resources as a development that fails (or fails to perform as well as it should) due to being disconnected, inaccessible, unwelcoming, unadaptable or inflexible.

The appraisal of the development should ask: Will the development use resources efficiently in construction and operation? This should be considered in context to orientation, drainage, energy, movement, waste, greenspace and current established standards. The following list of questions can be used to check that the use of resources has been considered fully, in line with the principles set out in policy documents such as CLG's *Planning Policy Statement: Planning and Climate Change* and *The Planning Response to Climate Change*.

The zinc-clad roofs of Rock House, overlooking Loch Tay in Scotland, mimic the profile of the thatched roofs of traditional longhouses. The external walls are clad in naturally weathering larch, the same timber as the surrounding trees. The building is oriented on a north-south axis, so that all the rooms benefit from solar gain both morning and evening. Completely airtight, the building is ventilated by a heat recovery system, the waste heat being transferred back to a heating accumulator tank.

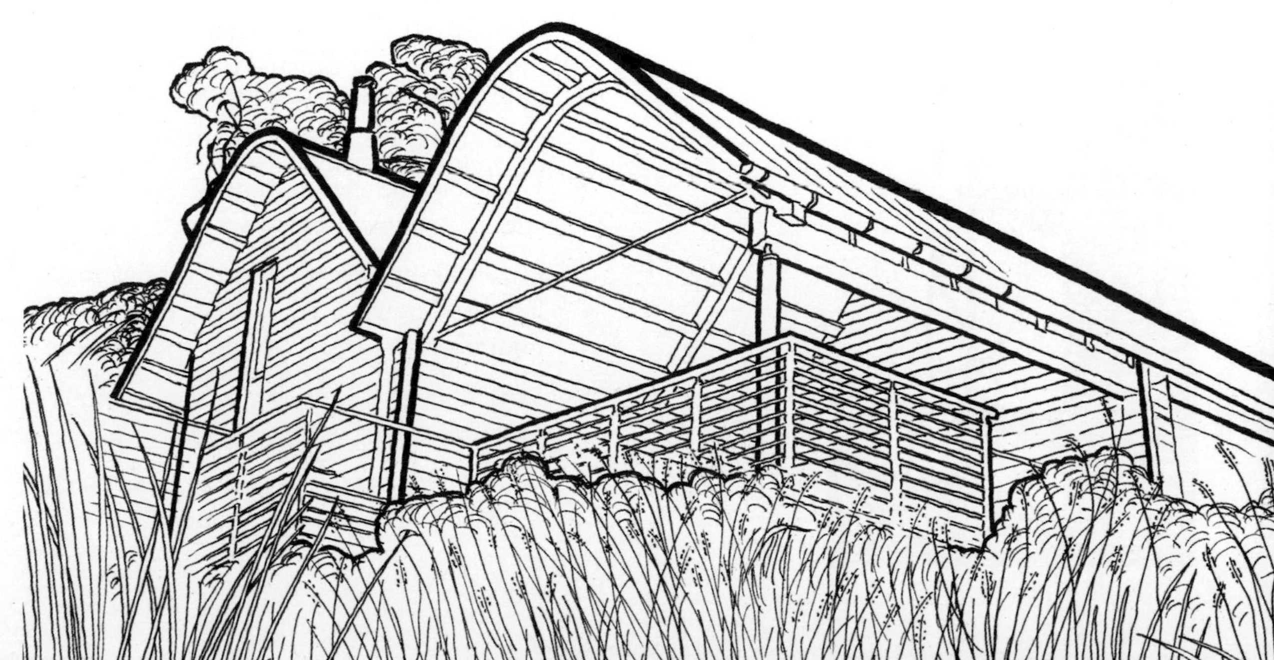

A scheme of 145 homes at Oxley Woods, Milton Keynes, was the first to be built under the Design for Manufacture competition. The structural and internal walls were constructed off-site. The government had challenged the development industry to build homes to a strict cost limit and high quality standards. Designed by architects Rogers Stirk Harbour and Partners, the houses have a high degree of airtightness and a heat recovery system.

A wind turbine on a newly built apartment block in east London.

RESOURCES AND EFFICIENCY: WHAT TO ASK

Orientation

- What is the site's main orientation?
- Will the development take advantage of passive solar gain?
- Will shading (trees or artificial shading) prevent summer overheating?
- Will the development take advantage of prevailing winds during warmer months and minimise wind-tunnel effects during cooler months?
- Are public spaces likely to have a pleasant micro-climate, without strong winds, glare or significant over-shadowing?
- Are the buildings designed to maximise the potential for passive solar gain?
- Are buildings designed for stack- and cross-ventilation?
- Are buildings designed to be sheltered from prevailing winds during the cooler months?

Energy

- Is there a site-wide energy strategy, based on an energy hierarchy approach (reducing the demand for energy; supplying as much as possible of the energy requirement from on-site renewable or low-carbon sources; and supplying as much as possible of the remaining demand from off-site low-carbon technologies, including decentralised and district sources)?
- How does the energy strategy relate to the energy strategy of the wider area?
- How will the energy demand for heating, lighting, hot water and cooling be minimised?
- Which renewable or low-carbon energy solutions will be used?
- What level of analysis has been undertaken to arrive at the proposed solutions?

Drainage

- Has a sustainable drainage system been prepared for the site? If so, is it integrated into the landscape?
- How will the development deal with storm and rainwater run-off?
- Is there a site-wide rainwater recycling proposal? If so, does it recycle used water or other sources of non-potable water?

Movement

- Will it be easy, safe and pleasant to walk or cycle to shops, surgeries, a library and other amenities? How long will it take?
- How will cycling and walking be promoted across the site and to neighbouring areas?
- How close will the development be to bus and rail services?
- How will residents be able to get to these transport options?
- What is the overall car parking ratio for the site? What will be done to reduce private car use and to promote other forms of transport?
- What provision is being made for a car club, car club parking spaces and electric car charging points?

Waste

- Has waste management for the site and within the buildings been considered adequately (including its visual impact)?
- Has adequate space been allocated for different recycling methods used now and likely to be used in the future?
- Will community-based waste collection systems be provided?
- Will the waste collection system avoid adverse impact on the public realm?
- Will automated waste collection systems or other site-wide waste solutions be used?
- Will arrangements be made and facilities be provided to collect separated waste streams?
- Will a construction waste strategy be developed to minimise waste to landfill from the site during clearance and construction?
- Is there a strategy eventually to achieve a zero-waste policy?

Greenspace

- Is there a greenspace strategy for the site?
- Will all residents be able to access green amenity space easily?
- Has greenspace been designed to facilitate walking and cycling across the site?
- Will a productive landscape be provided for food production?
- Will greenspace promote biodiversity?

Standards

- What level of the relevant environmental standard will be achieved? (For housing the standard for England and Wales is Code for Sustainable Homes, levels 1-6, and for Scotland Ecohomes, pass to excellent. For commercial development the standard is BREEAM, pass to outstanding.)
- Will privately owned and social housing be built to the same standard?

Out-of-town supermarkets encourage travel by car.

Case study
An alternative to suburban sprawl

Upton, on the edge of Northampton, has been designed as an urban extension, avoiding suburban sprawl. When it is complete, the neighbourhood will consist of more than 1,000 homes and a mix of other uses. The plan was developed through 'enquiry by design' exercises, bringing together the stakeholders in what would otherwise have been a much longer process.

The layout is based on a hierarchy of connected streets: the main street; streets with exposed sustainable drainage systems; ordinary streets; lanes (home zones); and mews. A design code specifies the characteristics of each. Pedestrians and vehicles share space in mews and courtyards. Each home is allocated a parking space in a back court. Unallocated spaces are provided on streets and mews.

Upton was initiated by the Homes and Communities Agency's predecessor English Partnerships with Northampton Borough Council and the Prince's Foundation.

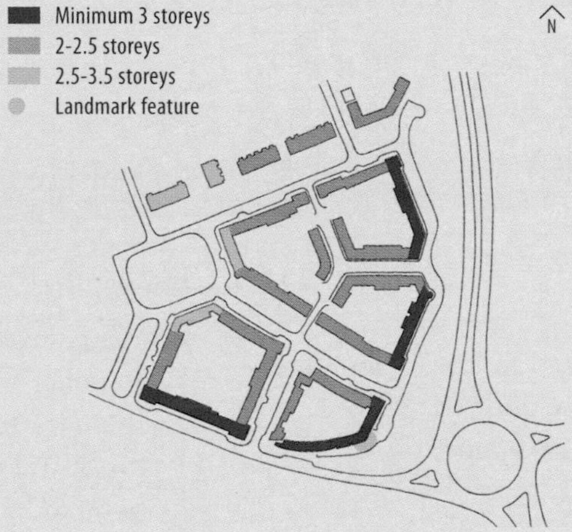

N

Despite the suburban location, Upton's designers have created streets with a distinctly urban form (far left). A sustainable drainage system in the widest streets (below) manages rainwater run-off in a way that reduces the risk of flooding. The green watercourses, crossed by pedestrian bridges, promote local biodiversity. The plan of Upton's first phase (left) shows building heights.

ASPECTS OF ARCHITECTURE AND TOWNSCAPE

Two modern reinterpretations of the traditional mews, at Upton (top) and Newbury Mews in Camden, London (above). The angled facades at Newbury Mews, combined with staggered balconies and frosted glass, avoid unacceptable overlooking, despite the houses' close proximity.

Architecture and townscape

Some of the objectives of planning relate to functional aspects of a development (how it will work) and some to aesthetic ones (how it will make us feel). These are usually closely related to one another. The feelings evoked by a development are perhaps a more subjective matter than the functional aspects of good design. To appraise a development proposal in these terms depends on understanding space and scale, and appreciating aesthetic qualities, drawing on expert opinion where necessary.

Deciding whether a proposed development is likely to be valued as a successful work of architecture (however modest) will involve relating the proposal to three considerations.

- First, what sort of design is accepted by the general public? This can be determined by consulting the public (though this may not be easy) or its representatives; or planners may feel that they know from experience what sort of design is generally publicly acceptable. But thinking about design should not stop there.
- The second question to ask is: what sort of design is accepted generally by the design community? This may be determined by consulting the local authority's own design advisors, whether in-house, consultants, or a local, regional or national design panel.
- A third, more difficult, question relates to innovative architecture. The question is: what may be accepted in the future as being excellent architecture and is currently accepted by design innovators of the avant-garde? Determining this may be helped by consulting specialists or design review panels consisting of people skilled in appraising architecture in unfamiliar forms. Even if these people disagree with one another, their discussions may be illuminating.

In appraising a development proposal, we need to consider how much weight to give to these respective opinions – of the public; of the local authority's design advisors; and of outside specialists. The democratic planning process has to consider conflicting opinions and arrive at a decision.

Before discussing how to think about architecture and townscape, we need to understand how the planning system currently considers such matters, and why that is the cause of considerable confusion.

'Character and appearance' (usually in that specific phrase) are overwhelmingly the terms that dominate planners' reports on planning applications and inspectors' decision reports on

EXAMPLE: A CITY LANDMARK AND A LOCAL PRESENCE

A building can have an impact at different scales, all of which need to be considered in the planning process. The office tower in the City of London designed by Foster Associates, known as the Gherkin, has an impact on people who work there and who visit it; on the area immediately around it; on its neighbourhood; and, as a landmark, on central London as a whole. Planners need to understand each of these potential impacts and, if there is any conflict between them, to appraise the relative importance of each.

The Gherkin has an impact at a range of scales.

planning appeals. But 'character' and 'appearance' seem often to be used with little thought, becoming little more than a catch-all for undigested opinions.

Before devising Qualityreviewer we examined 200 planning appeals from the year 2009, selected at random, to discover the role design and the physical form of development played in them. Using the inspector's decision letter from the Planning Casework Service or a report of the decision, we noted what the inspector in each case recorded as the significant relevant issues (apart from land use, which is a very common issue in planning appeals). In most cases more than one issue was mentioned.

Just over half the cited issues related to the proposed development's physical form and appearance. This highlights how important design issues are to the planning process. The table shows the number of mentions for the 18 most common issues.

THE ISSUES AT STAKE IN PLANNING APPEALS

Type of issue identified by the inspector	Number of mentions
Character and appearance	151
Architectural issues	44
Other physical aspects of development	36
Scale	28
Highway and movement issues	25
Vitality and vibrancy	25
Residential amenity	17
Highway safety	16
Sustainability (using that word)	14
Noise	13
Need	12
Openness	11
Economic benefit	6
Flood risk	5
Security	5
Views	5
Affordable housing	4
Safety	4

EXAMPLE: HOW DID THEY DESIGN FILLING STATIONS IN THE 15TH CENTURY?

A petrol filling station has been built in a historic Cotswolds village: a standard filling station design has been augmented with a pitched roof (below). Someone has given serious thought to the question: how did they design filling stations in the 15th century?

A carwash has been built in the lee of a 19th century gatehouse (right). The carwash has been faced with flint to match the 19th century gatehouse.

There is something ridiculous about both of these buildings. The laboured attempts to fit in make them stand out more than they might otherwise have done. In some cases a new building will compliment the old one successfully if it is distinctively different and carefully designed. Getting the design right involves not just choosing the right materials and designing the details thoughtfully, but thinking about where and how the new buildings are situated. Sometimes instead of asking whether this is the right design, a better question might be: is this the right place? The context might be better respected, and the new building might be more attractive, if it were on a different part of the site, or on a different site altogether.

Copying vernacular details may not be the best solution.

In discussing character and appearance in their decision letters, planning inspectors also used the following terms, among others: alienness, appropriateness, attractiveness, compatibility, conspicuousness, disfiguration, distinctiveness, incongruity, intrusiveness, obtrusiveness, visual amenity, visual anomaly, visual benefit, visual harm, visual impact, visual integration and visual quality. In discussing specifically architectural issues, they wrote of, among other terms: blandness, coalescence, coherence, cohesiveness, complementarity, configuration, consistency, discordancy, idiosyncracy, innovation, integration, interest, subservience, symmetry, ugliness, variety, verticality, visual dominance and visual harmony.

Character and appearance are important, but they are often given a prominence in the planning process that overshadows more fundamental – and often less subjective – attributes of a development proposal. Too often a superficial appraisal of character distorts a local authority's consideration of design quality.

Understanding the distinctive character of a place is essential in designing for that place or appraising a development proposal. But character is not something separate from a place's other attributes: it is made up of them. Understand a place in terms of movement and legibility, space and enclosure, mixed uses and tenures, adaptability and resilience, resources and efficiency, and architecture and townscape, and you have understood its distinctive character.

Design in the light of that understanding and you have designed development that will respect that character. Appraise a development proposal in terms of that understanding and you know all you need to know about the impact the development will have on the place's character.

Many of the issues that we see discussed in the planning process as relating to 'character' are aspects of the place's (or the design's) architecture and townscape. In this section Qualityreviewer discusses aspects of architecture and townscape that might be relevant in relation to a particular development proposal.

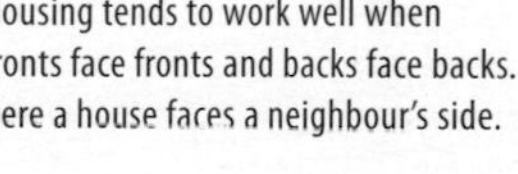
Housing tends to work well when fronts face fronts and backs face backs. Here a house faces a neighbour's side.

ASPECTS OF ARCHITECTURE AND TOWNSCAPE

Architecture and townscape

INTEGRATION

The most important question to ask of a development proposal in relation to architecture and townscape is: how successfully will the development be integrated into its setting?

A building becomes part of a place. It may have been consciously designed as part of the place, either skillfully or not. Many buildings, though, are not designed for the place, or hardly so. They may be designed by someone who is thinking only of the building itself, with little concern for context. Sometimes such a building may yet enhance the place, but it is unwise to leave this to luck.

Most developments – housing schemes, shopping malls, superstores or business parks, for example – look as if they could be anywhere, with nothing locally distinctive about them. In many cases they are built to the standard designs of nationwide or international organisations, fitted to the site with minimal adaptation.

A 19th century industrial building (seen on the far left of the drawing below) lies next to this new housing development in a historic northern city. Its existence has been used as an excuse to build a series of blocks of apartments, almost identical to one another, as if industrial-style dullness were a virtue in modern housing.

This new building in a mews street in Camden, London, presents a strikingly different form, but it uses traditional materials at the ground floor and maintains the building line. A wide variety of building forms and styles is a characteristic of this street.

Even when a planning proposal has been designed for a particular site, the planners – often prompted by local residents and their representatives – express concern about what they see as the scheme's failure to fit in. This raises two questions. First, how can the character of a place be appraised? Second, once it has been appraised, how should that character be reflected, if at all, in new development?

Sometimes the character of an area may not be something that anyone would want to emulate. The place may be extremely unattractive, and new development should set its sights higher. But the scale of existing development or a regular street pattern may provide clues about how to design new development. Or the site may be an almost featureless green field: in such cases there are almost always some aspects of the landscape, the micro-climate or the place's history, for example, that the designer needs to understand.

In some places this is easier than in others. In the world heritage city of Bath, for example, the local authority has identified the most characteristic features of the city's historic buildings. These are, it says, a limited palette of materials; the use of Bath stone and Welsh slate; the scale and consistency of natural materials; and the inherent colours of natural materials and their natural weathering.

Cotswold District Council has identified a 'Cotswold style'. This is characterised by steep-pitched roofs with ridge tiles and copings; tall chimneys; symmetrically balanced design with evenly spaced openings; large window sills of stone or wood; detailed window surrounds of stone; and no barge boards or eaves fascias. Many places, though, do not have such a strong, consistent or positive character.

A real understanding of the character of an area will depend on carrying out a careful context appraisal. What is most important about the place? Who lives here? What do they value about it? How and why does the place work? Some of the answers will relate to physical things that anyone observant (or, in some cases, with certain specialist

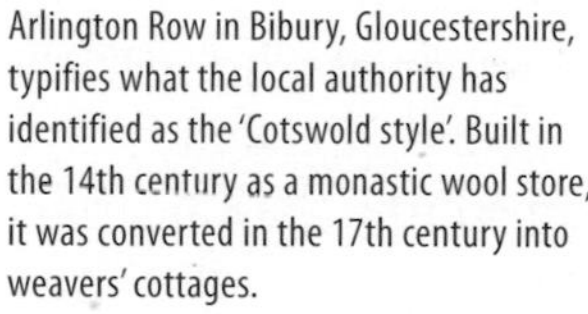

Arlington Row in Bibury, Gloucestershire, typifies what the local authority has identified as the 'Cotswold style'. Built in the 14th century as a monastic wool store, it was converted in the 17th century into weavers' cottages.

Part of a new shop, the building on the right is meant to reflect the character of its Victorian neighbour, but the details jar. These are not real windows and the black glass is opaque.

knowledge) will notice. Other answers will relate to the life of the place, and only people who know it well will be able to provide the answers.

Having identified the local character, the next question is how to respond to it. It may be more important to get the big things right, such as matching the local pattern of street blocks and plots, and linking into the local network of routes, than to copy some detail of the local style or vernacular (see page 84).

A combination of copying some local detail while failing to understand the most important characteristics can lead to a new development looking absurd – as, for example, when some features of the design of local cottages are reproduced on buildings of a different use and much larger scale. A thoughtless appeal to local character is often the first resort of a lazy designer.

Few of the historic places that we enjoy visiting have developed according to anyone's idea of what character should be created or perpetuated. People generally built whatever seemed right at the time: whatever served their business, appealed to their taste or presented them to the world – and matched their budget. They did all this in a specific local context.

All but a few of the medieval buildings in a city might have been replaced in the Georgian era. Many of the Georgian buildings may have been replaced by Victorian buildings, at a larger scale. The result is, perhaps, a delightful mess: a place with character, but not a simple character that could be described easily.

Careful analysis would show, though, that despite the different circumstances of people who built at various times, there were influences in common. These might include a cold prevailing wind that buildings needed to be sheltered from; certain building materials that were easily available; or a particular way the land sloped and the relationship of that with the direction of the sun.

Today matters are very different. Houses may be built by national house builders, whose products may be the same everywhere, despite being given token regional names. Shopping malls may be developed by international companies who specialise in building such things. Shops may be parts of national or international chains, following a design issued from headquarters in London, or Arkansas, or somewhere else.

Where once the scale of buildings was limited by the technologies of brick, stone and timber, today's technology allows building at dramatically larger scales. Where once the patterns of routes were determined largely by how far people could walk, modern transport technologies have eroded that dimension. By the time the design has accommodated the need to park cars, and provide storage and recycling of large amounts of rubbish, the scope for designing to a local pattern or style seems very limited. Standard solutions tend to be replicated nationwide.

The challenge for planning is to promote thoughtful development that creates places with meaning.

The main living space of this house in Brecon, Wales, is cantilevered towards the river. The timber and steel frame structure is clad with Welsh slate and local stone. Resource-saving features include high thermal mass, grass roofs, solar panels, wood-chip boiler and recycled grey water.

EXAMPLE: A POSITIVE CONTRIBUTION TO THE STREET SCENE

This, the headquarters of a City law firm, is a monster of a building, expressing the power of the corporate world. But at street level some clever design makes a positive contribution to the street scene. The new building continues the street frontage of the historic structure without copying its form. Enough of the Victorian building's lines are continued to integrate the new and the old, but the new is different enough to avoid destroying the old building's distinctiveness. There is no doubt where the entrance is.

The urban block (left); and the street frontage and its historic neighbour (right).

The planners had wanted stylistic details of this street's houses (left) to be copied in the new house on the corner site (above). As built, though, the house lacked those details. The front door, for example, is flat-topped (below right), unlike others in the street (below).

Case study
The details are not the heart of the problem

The local authority gave planning permission for a house that it thought would fit in with the others in this area of largely inter-war suburban housing. The permission was for a house with some of the features found elsewhere in the area, including quoins, an arched front door, a projecting two-storey bay with windows containing small panes, and mock-Tudor panel detailing on the bay above the first-floor window. When the house was built without these details, the local authority took enforcement action. The inspector agreed that although this was neither a conservation area nor did it possess any other special design designation, these details were needed 'to make the new building fit in'.

In the inspector's view 'the appeal scheme has its own distinctive character as a modern development which, in my opinion, should not necessarily seek to mimic the nearby inter-war period development.' But, he wrote, 'because of its prominent position in the street scene… I consider that the design of the development should contain design elements which reflect the character of the area.' The distinction between 'seeking to mimic', on the one hand, and 'containing design elements which reflect the character of the area', on the other, seems a subtle one in this case.

The inspector decided that the appellant must submit a proposal to the local planning authority specifying 'the precise details of the "mock-Tudor" panel; the colour of the external render; and the type and colour of the brick to be used in the brick quoins and the arched head to the front doorway.' When this was done, he wrote, the house 'would respect its surroundings and contribute positively to the character of the area'.

Adding those details, if it is ever done, may make the new house a little less conspicuous, but it will look like an uninspiring building with some bits stuck on.

The most distinctive quality of the neighbouring inter-war houses is that they are mature examples of their time. Would it not have been better to have built a good twenty-first century house rather than add an inferior attempt at an inter-war design? No doubt, but good new architecture is rare, and the planners may have had no reason to hope that this site was going to benefit from thoughtful design.

The inspector also insisted that details of hard and soft landscaping, including the design of the fences, should be agreed with the local planning authority.

What is wrong with the building is not that it lacks quoins, a mock-Tudor panel and an arched doorway, but that it shows no sign of having been designed for its site. The site is narrow and on a slope, with roads on three sides. Instead of backing on to other back gardens, as is usual with much semi-detached suburban housing, the back of the house faces the street and the front of one of the bungalows in an adjacent close.

As its site is higher than that of the bungalows, the new house appears particularly dominant. This makes the unattractiveness of the rear elevation all the more unfortunate. One of its features is a horizontal bathroom window, which may be the world's narrowest. Local residents supporting the enforcement action described this window as 'incongruous'. The inspector agreed that the window was 'a slightly unusual insertion', but he ruled that as 'an insignificant element in the rear elevation' its impact would be 'minimal'.

The fact that the new house's site has roads on three sides (top) would have been an interesting challenge to a skilled designer. The rear elevation (right) is particularly dominant and unattractive.

ASPECTS OF ARCHITECTURE AND TOWNSCAPE

Architecture and townscape

SCALE

If we need a measure of scale to use in designing development, we have one at hand. This is the human being: our size, the speed at which we walk, cycle or wheel ourselves, and the distance we can walk comfortably. Among the most important considerations of any design will be the scale of the street, the block, the plot, the section and the building's details.

People are different sizes, they walk at different speeds and they can walk different distances, but we can take those matters into account. The human scale lets us consider whether some feature of a building will seem smaller or large close at hand, friendly or intimidating, and whether it will be comfortable to walk near.

Some developments look as though they were designed with people on foot in mind, and to experience from close up. Others look as though (and in many cases were) designed to be viewed from passing motor vehicles, or as distant landmarks. In other cases the development shows no sign of having been designed with a thought of how it might relate to any particular scale at all. The best-designed development shows evidence of having been considered at the full range of scales (see example on page 62).

Drawings are static, but buildings are usually seen by people who are in motion. Observers, walking, cycling or driving, generally see the building as part of a streetscape or townscape: a series of doors, windows, roofs and other building elements, whole buildings, groups of buildings, and spaces which they pass by. The rhythm that the observer experiences, sometimes regular and sometimes irregular, may be pleasurable or it may be dull.

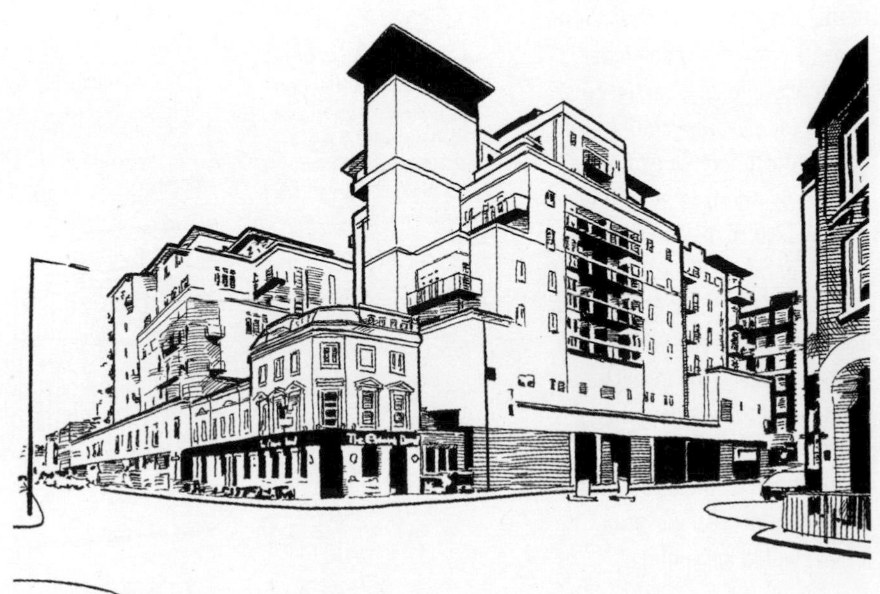

The Pimlico Village development in London is dramatically more massive than its older neighbours. Its visual impact depends on where it is seen from. Some people passing quite close by may hardly notice it. To others it is a dominant feature of the townscape.

EXAMPLE: THE URBAN RHYTHM BROKEN WITH A DULL THUD

The gables and narrow plots of these buildings on the market square of a town on the River Thames create a pleasing scale and rhythm. The building above Toni and Guy disrupts it. There is no reason, perhaps, why this building should not be higher than its neighbours: one of the attractions of historic places is often the rich mix of building styles, materials and sizes. There might be a justification for a landmark building on this prominent site.

Unfortunately little thought seems to have been given to the design. Brickwork; standard windows; a mansard roof to pretend that the top storey does not really exist: that is all.

A thoughtless disruption of the rich mix.

Case study
It's an uncomfortable squeeze

The density of this suburban area has been intensified over the years by development in large back gardens. Now a developer has spotted four gardens into which six more houses could be squeezed. A new drive will provide access to four of them. The four relate to one another awkwardly and fail to create any pleasant space.

The drive is unlikely to feel either clearly private or public. It opens up the backs of the existing houses to semi-public space in a way that often causes security problems, and will probably be lined with unattractive high timber fences. The development's design statement claims that the new homes will hardly be visible from the older neighbouring houses, being screened by bushes and trees. How dense will that foliage be? Can we be sure that the trees will not be cut down when the residents of the new houses find they take their light?

The local authority decided that this scheme would not create a pleasant place, and refused the planning application.

ASPECTS OF ARCHITECTURE AND TOWNSCAPE

Architecture and townscape

LAYOUT

The plan of the site or building is usually the first diagram that the architect or other designer draws when designing a development. The layout determines most of the movement that the development will allow. It shows how people will be able to move from space to space, and how they will access the building or buildings.

A plan shows the relationship between one part of the development and another: where the most important spaces are; how the other spaces serve them; the relationship between more public and more private spaces; and the relationship to exterior spaces. If the plan is well thought out, the development is likely to be more successful. It will support its intended functions, it will be accessible to the full range of people who want to use it, and it will make good use of its site. We need to consider, though, how the development may serve differing interests (those of the public and those of the client, for example) to varying degrees.

The section, another basic diagram of a building or development, adds a further dimension. Sections show relationships between elements of a building or development in terms of heights. In particular they help us think about the building in relation to the human scale, including how internal and external spaces will feel to people moving through them. Sections give clues to likely levels of privacy, and how adaptable to a range of uses the building might be. For example, residential accommodation with a tall ground floor may be easily convertible to commercial uses in the future.

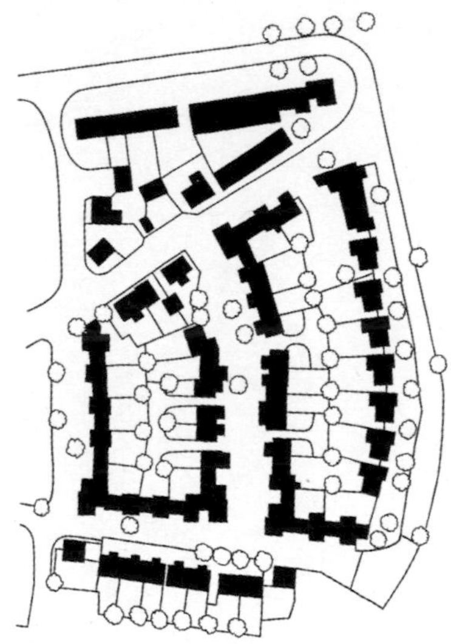

A plan of part of Newhall in Harlow, Essex, one of whose streets is illustrated on the front cover of this book.

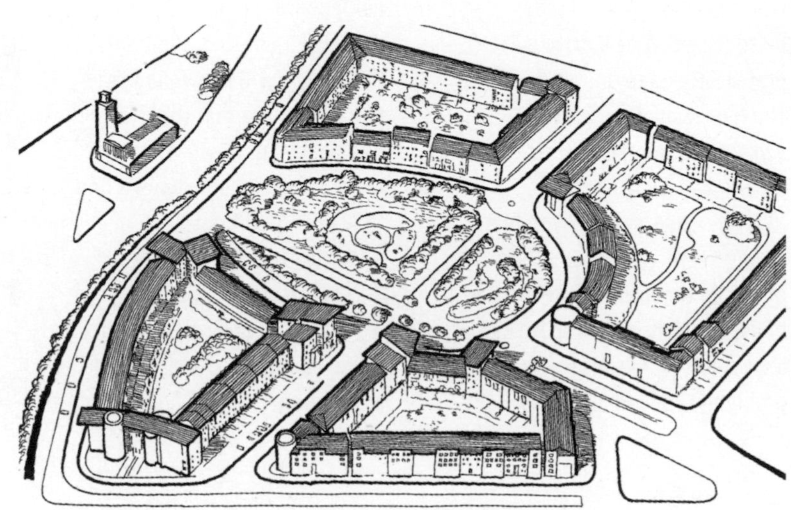

The fronts of the apartments in the Crown Street regeneration area (see page 45) face the street. The backs face space that is inaccessible to non-residents.

The backs of these houses face the street. This contributes to the impression that the street itself is just the back of something, rather than being a place of any value. Were these houses deliberately designed like that, with the idea that the residents would open up their patio doors and let the fumes in? Or were these standard house types that just happened to have patio doors?

A section can also show the relationship of the floor level of the proposed building to the ground level outside. A raised ground floor may create a degree of privacy, whereas a floor at ground level may provide greater visual or physical connection between inside and outside. A successful design will take account of the use of the building, the amount of private space at the front and the need to provide easy access.

Street sections show the most important relationships between elements of a street. They help us to judge how the height of the buildings will relate to the width of the street, how this compares with other streets with which we are familiar, and how tightly enclosed or open this will make the street feel. They help us to understand the extent to which space will be overlooked (which tends to make public space feel safer, whereas a high level of overlooking into private space can be either good or bad, depending on the ownership and control of the space).

EXAMPLE: HOUSES THAT TURN THEIR BACKS ON THE STREET

This house would offer a more attractive view to the south London street if it fronted on to it. Its front door and windows would have given the sense that the street was overlooked, and that people were coming and going. Instead the house presents its back, giving the impression that the street is the back of something and unlikely to be a place with any attractive qualities. Backing on to a street rather than on to another back garden makes a house less safe. That explains the razor wire, which makes the street feel less welcoming and safe.

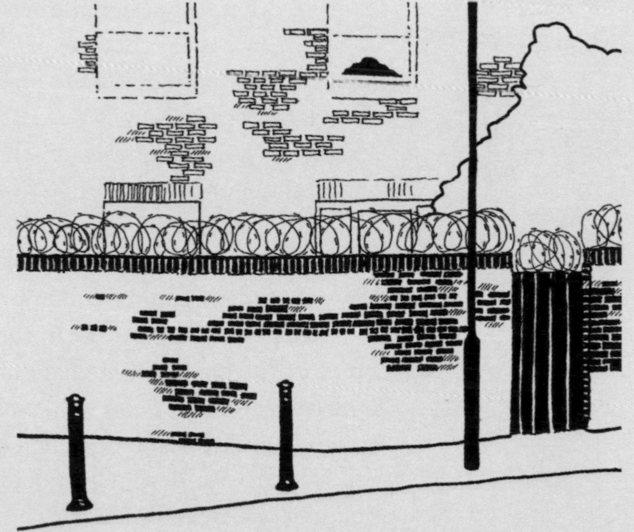

The razor wire is a desperate solution to the problem caused by the houses' failure to face the street.

Architecture and townscape

EXPRESSION AND HONESTY

Successful architecture communicates the designer's sense of what is harmonious and what will work well. The design may also make clear what the building's function is. If it does, it may be helping to make the place seem more friendly, welcoming and interesting.

Some buildings work well even though they do not express their function. Buildings in a Georgian terrace may have started as houses and been converted to offices or consulting rooms, without that being particularly noticeable. When designing development today, it may work well to decide the basic form of the buildings before allocating the specific uses. In an adaptable development, a building's first use may not be known when it is designed, and this use may be expected to change quite soon.

There may also be other occasions where it is appropriate not to display a building's functions. The architecture of pretence has a long and proud tradition. We need to ask whether this is one such occasion.

Too often, though, buildings miss the opportunity to communicate what they are, as though passers-by have no right to understand and enjoy the place where they find themselves.

Making clear how it is constructed is another way in which a building can communicate. The designer chooses how much to reveal about the building's construction, and how much to conceal for aesthetic reasons. The best architecture achieves a subtle balance between the two. Being aware of this can be a step towards understanding and appreciating the design.

Most buildings will form the background fabric of the place. Some of the best designed are modest and not immediately noticeable, but they can still contribute significantly to the place's quality. Other buildings will be designed to be noticed, giving full scope to the designer's talent for expression – whether the building is civic, religious or commercial, and public or private.

The Pier Arts Centre in Stromness, Orkney, Scotland, is a refurbishment and extension of listed buildings. The form of the original houses and boat sheds has been retained, while modern materials and details highlight the presence of an important cultural organisation.

EXAMPLE: ONE BUILDING, THREE FACADES, THREE CHARACTERS

Is this dishonest design? No, it is a traditional approach to townscape design, matching facades to their context.

The brief was to design a building with three frontages. One was on the great street of Piccadilly, adjoining a listed modernist building. The second frontage faced a listed Christopher Wren church. A third was on the elegant Jermyn Street, where rich people buy their shirts. The architect's response was to give each facade a distinct character.

The Piccadilly facade is suitably brash, emphasising, by contrast, the retrained character of its modernist neighbour. To the other neighbour, the brick Wren church, the building offers a more restrained, brick facade. On Jermyn Street the building turns stone again, but with the restrained elegance of a Turnbull and Asser shirt rather than the panache of Piccadilly. For the building's interior, the developer used another architect and another style, exchanging the exteriors' classicism for cool modernism.

Could the building have been designed as effectively in a modern style? Certainly, and it would be interesting to see how a talented architect would have managed it. Whatever the style, success would depend on the skill of the design team. In the wrong hands, designing in such a varied context could produce a real mess.

A view of the building from Piccadilly (left), with the listed modernist building to the left (the Wren church is to the right); and from Jermyn Street (above).

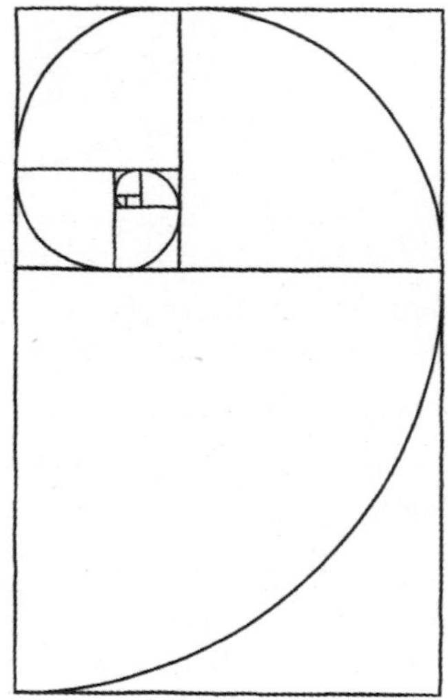

A diagram showing the proportions of the golden section.

A pair of semi-detached houses marred by windows of horizontal rather than vertical shape.

Architecture and townscape

PROPORTION

Most buildings are made up of regular shapes and volumes: walls, doors and windows, rooms and other internal spaces. Some arrangements of these shapes and volumes – the ratio between heights and widths, and proportions between solid and void, elements and facade – are generally agreed to be more pleasing than others.

Some people – including modernist as well as classical architects – go so far as to say that a particular proportion, the golden section (also known as the golden ratio and the golden mean) – is objectively the most beautiful. The golden section is based on a line divided so that the ratio of the smaller to the larger part is the same as the ratio of the larger part to the whole. At least one recent design guide for a major development calls for the proportions of the more prominent buildings to approximate to the golden section. The symbol of the Royal Town Planning Institute, adopted within the past decade, is based on a diagram of the golden section.

Most people consider that some arrangements of proportion are more pleasing than others, and that some people are better able to judge which these are, as a result of training or experience. Relying on the golden section is no easy answer, though, as judgement is still needed to guide the use of these proportions and such matters as arrangements of elements in the facade.

Building elements with vertical (as opposed to square and horizontal) proportions have a long tradition of creating pleasing buildings. This may relate to matters of land ownership (short frontages), structural efficiency (short spans for door and window lintels) and the fact that most doors – often the most important element in a building's facade – are of a vertical shape.

Proportion is not just a matter of two dimensions. The depth of a building element – a window or the eaves, for example – will have a significant influence of its appearance.

Judgements about proportion are to some extent subjective. People with good understanding of the matter may have differing views. This does not mean that it is just a matter of opinion. People with a deep knowledge of architecture will tend to agree about some of the essentials.

If a person carrying out a design appraisal does not feel confident in making aesthetic judgements, they will want to look for evidence of such matters having been given careful thought by skilled designers.

EXAMPLE: AN UNINSPIRING SOLUTION TO A TOWNSCAPE CHALLENGE

This site in the city of London faced the office building's designers with some interesting challenges. How does the building relate to the circus and the two streets leading into it? How can the design provide interest from close up and from further away? How will parts of the building relate to the whole? How can the location of the entrance be made clear?

The designers seem to have been baffled and to have avoided the challenges. An architectural feature has been added to the third and fourth floors for no evident reason.

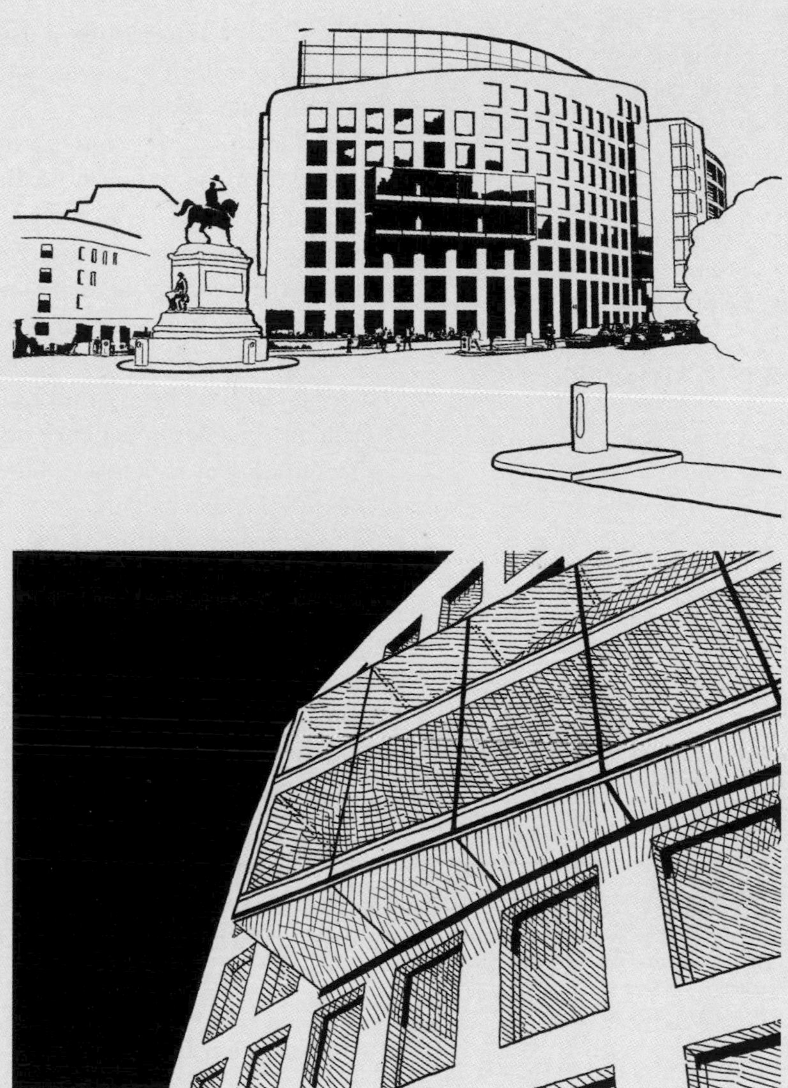

Here was an opportunity to make a great contribution to the townscape, but the building makes little of it.

The Scottish baronial style has provided inspiration for buildings large (above) and small (centre), but the effect is lost if the proportion and details are wrong (right).

Architecture and townscape

ORDER

One of the characteristics of good design is what can be called order. This is itself made up of three other characteristics: balance, repetition and symmetry.

A large part of design is a matter of creating relationships between parts and the whole. Balance is a satisfying sense that the relationship is right. It is very different from something mechanical or natural: although it may be difficult to define, it is clearly the result of someone knowing intuitively what will work, or trying out alternatives until they find the most pleasing.

Repetition, the second of our attributes of order, again makes a design distinct from something in the natural world. Repeating elements in a design will not necessarily add to the attractiveness of a building or streetscape, but repetition is one of the devices that the designer can call on.

Symmetry is a third means of bringing order to a building plan or to a facade. Again, it is a device to be used where appropriate.

A respect for order does not imply that a building can not be a landmark or that a place should not have landmark buildings.

Classical architecture was, and is, a method based on order. Balance, repetition, symmetry and the classical orders themselves (Doric, Ionic, Corinthian, Tuscan and Composite, among others) are used in creating architectural order.

Today, when relatively few buildings are designed in a classical style, the concept of order is still likely to be at the heart of a designer's approach. Some of the most celebrated modernist buildings (whose principles shunned many historic principles of design) have used new materials and methods in an almost classical sense of order. Looking for balance, repetition and symmetry may be a useful step in understanding the designer's intentions and the degree to which they have been fulfilled, whatever the style.

Opened in 2009, the fire station in the Prince of Wales' model community at Poundbury, Dorchester, is an attempt to match a historic style to a modern function.

A prominent landmark in Gateshead, the Baltic Flour Mill was built in the 1940s and converted to an arts centre in the 1990s. Its bulk has been used as a precedent to build a cluster of apartment blocks which vaguely reflect the mill's form, detracting from the original building's impressive effect.

ASPECTS OF ARCHITECTURE AND TOWNSCAPE

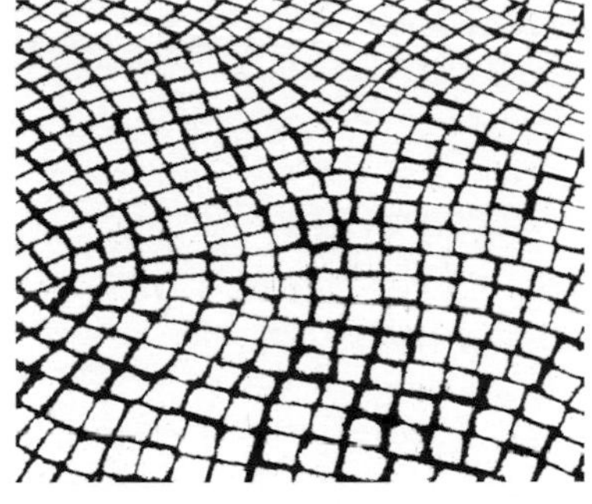

Paving with setts: designers need to consider appearance, ease of movement and maintenance, among other issues.

Architecture and townscape

MATERIALS

The materials of which a development is constructed will influence whether it can be resourced from recycled materials, what distance any new materials will have to be brought, whether the development can be built with local labour, how much energy and carbon dioxide its construction will represent, what it looks like, what it will feel like to touch, how visible it will be, how reflective it will be, how interesting it will be to look at, how liable it will be to staining, and how easy it will be to clean.

The materials will influence how easy the development will be to heat, how cool it will be in summer, how weatherproof it will be, how much rainfall will run off, who can walk or wheel themselves across its spaces comfortably, and how easy it will be for people with poor sight to find their way around. They will influence how much energy the development will take to heat or cool, whether it gives off toxic fumes, how easy it will be to maintain, how well it will age, whether it will blend in or differentiate itself from its context, how easy it will be to adapt, how much it will cost over its lifetime, how long it will last, how easy it will be to demolish or dismantle, and how easy it will be to recycle.

EXAMPLE: RELATIVE VALUES IN A WORLD HERITAGE SITE

Building in a place of valued townscape (and most townscape is valued to some extent) raises the question of how to respond to what is already there. This is nowhere more true than in Bath, where the whole city is a world heritage site.

The Thermae Bath Spa development, completed in 2006, uses the distinctive, honey-coloured Bath stone, among other materials, but does not copy the Georgian style of architecture. The planners' aim is to let the city change, while maintaining its distinctive character and the coherence of its appearance.

The Thermae Bath Spa development, completed in 2006, uses the traditional Bath stone but does not adopt a Georgian style of architecture.

EXAMPLE: AN UNFRIENDLY FACE TO THE STREET

For years this site on this busy south London road was filled by a collapsing lean-to extension. Its replacement provides an office downstairs and apartment above. The height of the development was constrained by the fact that the building on the left has windows at first-floor level which could not be obscured.

It is good to see the designer working in a modern idiom, even if the result – in grey-painted steel – looks rather industrial. The building gives no clue to passers by as to what its uses are. Its most striking feature, though, is not the appearance of the building itself, but the defensive impression given by the wall and high fence. The street's most attractive characteristic is perhaps the small front gardens (saved by being too small to pave over and park on) and low walls. The new building's designer appears not to have noticed.

The high fence is the infill scheme's most obtrusive element.

Architecture and townscape

DETAIL

Urban designers sometimes say that the detail of a building is less important than how it fits into the structure of the place: how it is laid out, and how it relates to patterns of movement and of plots and blocks. It is true that these are the most significant and longest-lasting elements. They may survive, as they often have done in historic places, while individual buildings come and go. The medieval high street may no longer have any medieval buildings, but it may still be the main feature of the town's layout. These elements will help determine in large part how people can move about.

The massing (the overall shape of the buildings) will also be a big influence on how the place feels. This is why some early planning and design decisions are often taken on the basis of looking at block models, which show the layout and the massing, but none of the detail.

Unfortunately the design of some development seems not to have benefited from much thought beyond the block-model stage. Yet the development's impact on people who use it and experience it will be influenced significantly by the detail: by the skill applied to its detailed design, by what the building is made of, by how its parts fit together, and by the care with which it is built.

The human experience of buildings and of architecture is partly a response to the work of human hand and mind. Buildings that reflect thought and care contribute to making a place seem human and friendly.

The railings outside a new office building in London provide some interest at street level.

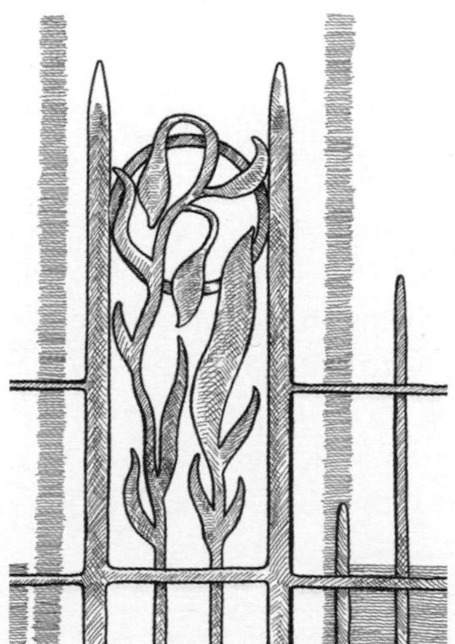

A carefully detailed apartment block at Accordia, Cambridge (see page 88), built with structural green oak frames.

ASPECTS OF ARCHITECTURE AND TOWNSCAPE

This reinterpretation of the form of an ancient temple has a practical function. Designed by the architect John Outram, the brightly coloured building on London's Isle of Dogs is a water pumping station. The stubby columns flanking the entrance contain ventilation ducts, and the roundel in the pediment has a fan to expel methane.

Tudor House in Romsey, Hampshire, reflects local building practices and the technology of its time.

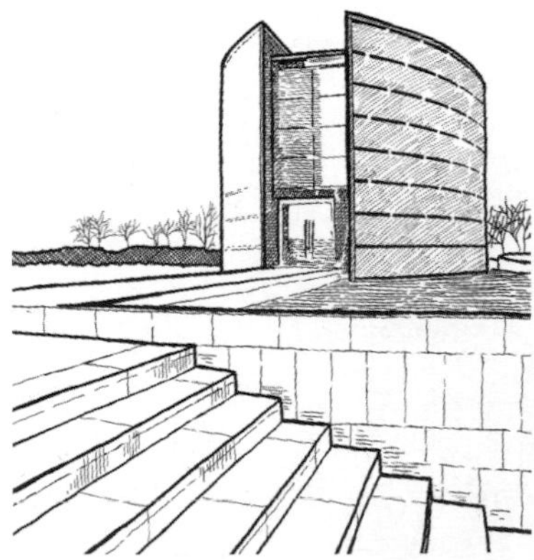

The Ruskin Library at Lancaster University was designed by the architect Sir Richard MacCormac as a symbolic gateway to the university. The exterior's simplicity contrasts with the richness of the interior.

Architecture and townscape

STYLE

Most great architects, like any other great artists, have a uniquely distinctive style. Most other architects (and most other designers of buildings) are inspired by them, at least to some extent. They design in a manner that in years to come will be datable fairly precisely to a particular time when that style was in fashion. There may be some relatively timeless architectural styles, such as certain varieties of classicism, classic modernism or vernacular, but most buildings reveal the time when they were designed and built.

There is not necessarily anything wrong with that. But in designing and appraising buildings we must be aware that what seems fresh and novel today may soon look dated. What will be valued in the future will be evidence of the care, thought and creativity that has gone into the design.

A building does not have to be designed in any specific style (though there is probably nothing that a critic could not put a label to, even if it is only 'functionalism'). There is nothing as delightful as a building that has been thoughtfully designed and carefully built with the unselfconscious threefold aims of fulfilling its function, enhancing the place and looking good.

Of buildings that are designed in a specific, identifiable style, the most common include vernacular, classical and modernist. Other styles include buildings whose appearance expresses aspects of low-carbon technologies.

VERNACULAR

Buildings that emulate local vernacular styles will incorporate or interpret the form and details of local traditional buildings. This can be done well or badly.

At its worst, this approach can lead to a detail or two being mindlessly copied, without capturing any of the essential character of the original. Traditional details may have been a response to some particular local condition, such as the availability of building materials or the local climate, which is no longer a constraint on building today. Or they may have been a local stylistic device, used by particular people at a particular time. In either case, copying them superficially may add little to the attractiveness of the new building and may even detract from the distinctiveness of the old. Vernacular details used at a very different scale or in an inappropriate context can look ridiculous.

At its best, though, emulating local vernacular styles can capture something of the distinctiveness of the place, and enhance it.

Classical style used carefully in a 1980s office development at Richmond Riverside in London (above); crudely in a south London apartment building (below); and imaginatively reinvented for an international bank in London (bottom).

CLASSICISM

Buildings that are designed in a classical style will copy or reinvent classical forms and details: pediments, columns, pilasters, quoins, friezes, cornices and so on. Their designers may do this in a way that classicists consider to be true to the spirit of the original. The design may be based on a good understanding of the language of classical architecture and it may get the grammar right. In other cases the attempt to adapt a historic style to new conditions will fail. The building may look ill-conceived rather than successfully drawing on a valued architectural tradition.

MODERNISM

Buildings designed in a modernist style are likely to have little or no ornamentation, but the quality of detailing is as important as in any other style. Sometimes a modernist style is used as an excuse for lack of thought about how the building is detailed. In that case the result will be a dull, plain building.

For a modernist building to look good, every element must be carefully designed, including how the materials are chosen and treated, and how one element meets another. The quality of thought may be evident from the drawings, but the quality of the finished building will also depend on how well it is built. The line between dull plainness and exquisite simplicity is often a fine one.

Some modernist buildings look as though they have been designed with little regard for the site, the neighbouring buildings or the place. Others successfully respond to their context, enhancing the streetscene without copying their neighbours' styles.

EXAMPLE: WHEN BIG IS NOT BEAUTIFUL

A big office building in this south London town centre overshadows its neighbours. There is not necessarily anything wrong with that. This is where the nineteenth century meets the twenty-first and the town centre meets the suburb. The local authority's planning policy states that higher densities are appropriate in this location that is very well connected by public transport.

What is unfortunate about this building is not its scale, but its crude massing and lack of detailing. The overbearing building dominates the street without contributing anything of interest either to distant views or to the experience of people passing by.

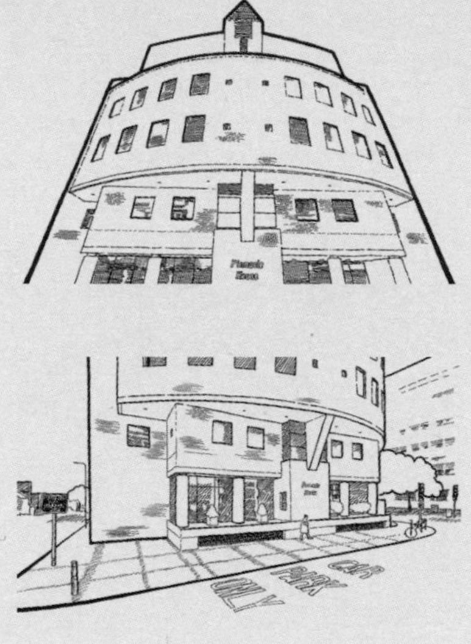

A dull building whichever way you look at it.

Quirkiness works best when tempered with thoughtfulness and creative flair. There is little evidence of either here.

EXAMPLE: IT'S NOT THAT WINDOWS HAVE TO BE RECTANGULAR...

One building in a terrace of houses has been refaced and reconfigured to provide two small offices, one upstairs and one down, each with its own door. There is no reason why windows must be rectangular, or why a new use in a different century should not create a building that looks very different to the rest of the street of Victorian houses.

But it needs a great deal of thought and creative flair to do it well, and there is little evidence of either here. The parts of the building – the windows, the doors and the cornice line – seem to relate neither to each other nor to the neighbouring houses.

EXAMPLE: GOOD MANNERS AND A SPARK OF LIFE

This is a prominent site in Inverness: a street on the south bank of the river Ness, facing the city centre. The new two-storey building is a restaurant. Usually in such a setting a new building would be in the vernacular style or something carefully contextual. This, though, is boldly modern: a glass frontage, two steel columns and an ogee-curved roof. For all its modernist style, the building respects its context with its narrow plot, vertical emphasis and lively addition to the street's varied roofline. It is not just a frontage: the building looks good, and coherent, from the back as well.

This delightful building would have been even better if the builders had managed to construct a more even double curve, or if the joint where the two columns meet their base had been more elegantly designed. But those details do not spoil the effect.

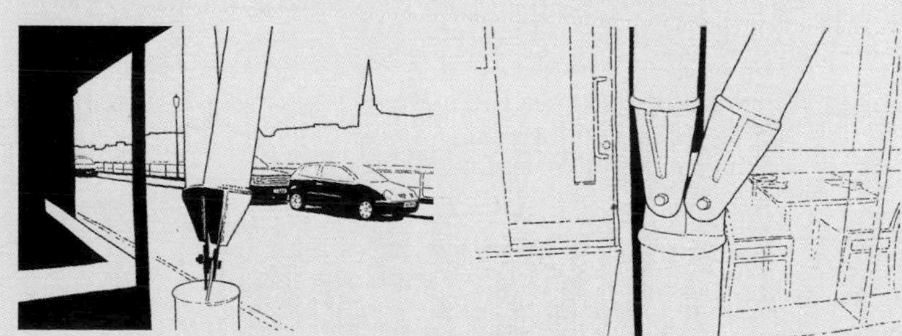

The restaurant building seen from across the river (top); from the front and back; in the context of the street (right); and two views of the point where the columns meet (bottom).

Case study
Creative design can involve breaking the rules

Accordia in Cambridge is the only housing development to have been awarded the Stirling Prize for architecture. It has been awarded several other design prizes as well. This is highly unconventional housing design. Building it was very painful for the companies that were the initial builders and developer, but that has been forgotten. It seems a pleasant place to live, the open areas are well kept and the houses sell for high prices.

It is not surprising that Accordia has won design prizes. Most housing developments have very little thought given to their design, being more or less standard arrangements of standard units. The housing at Accordia has had a great deal of thought given to it. A masterplan created an unusual layout (see page 35: the designers describe the concept as 'urban rugs on a carpet of landscape'). Many of the house types show evidence of their designers starting almost from scratch in thinking about what a house should be. Some of the houses have unusual and ingenious arrangements of terraces, internal courtyards and roof gardens.

Accordia has several features that in other places have tended not to work well. The scheme has only one link to the road network for vehicles, making it an enclave rather than a connected part of the city. Most of the housing association accommodation, located at the south end of the site, furthest

from the entrance, is visibly less well detailed compared with the market housing.

Some of the houses have living rooms that face directly on to public open space. Others have fronts (or backs: it is not quite clear which is which) that face on to shared open space. This space, shared between the houses, is intended to promote interaction and a feeling of community between the residents. It is also publicly accessible through an unlocked gate and a low fence. Such ambiguous, semi-private spaces are often unsuccessful, and sometimes end up being gated, where this is possible.

Whether Accordia's potential weaknesses will ever cause problems remains to be seen. The residents have a great deal invested in their homes and every incentive to protect the area's quality. A development that might fail in one setting – where there are high levels of anti-social behaviour, perhaps – might succeed in another. There is no need for every development to be equally robust.

Reviewing a planning proposal should involve identifying potential weaknesses and judging whether they are likely to be significant in the light of all the other circumstances. The best designs surprise us by succeeding in ways that we did not imagine – which is why we tend to trust in creative designers, not in designing-by-numbers.

Accordia makes the most of the site's many mature trees (top). Some living rooms front on to shared space (opposite page). People and cars share space on the mews streets (below).

EXAMPLE: GEOMETRY – BUT NOT AS WE KNOW IT

The humanities and social science graduate centre for Queen Mary, University of London, incorporates a former lock-keeper's cottage. The university's website explains that the design of the original cottage, built in 1820, was 'simple, practical and quickly built' – as if to establish that the old building was not of such great historical or architectural significance that the new construction need appear subservient to it. Indeed, the new building completely overpowers the cottage. It is bold, brash and colourful, with wildly different geometry. It is a building that wants to be noticed, projecting an exciting image to young people who it hopes will choose to study there.

The style is not wholly original. The new graduate centre is reminiscent of another graduate centre – that of London Metropolitan University, designed by the celebrated architect Daniel Libeskind, and also of his extraordinary deconstructionist design (which was granted planning permission but remains unbuilt due to lack of money) for an extension to London's V&A museum.

The architects have attempted to describe the Queen Mary building in lectures and articles. The language they tend to use is abstract and somewhat baffling. But buildings can often be enjoyed even when their designers find them hard to explain. People who enjoy this sort of building will share its architects' fascination with the self-imposed problem of how to match the functions normally accommodated by vertical, horizontal and rectangular elements to very different forms and angles.

The building's context is more complicated than just the nineteenth-century cottage. On one side of the building is the canal. On the other side is a new square, designed by the same architects, and a complex of large modern buildings.

The graduate centre for Queen Mary, University of London, incorporating a former lock-keeper's cottage.

ARCHITECTURE AND TOWNSCAPE: WHAT TO ASK

INTEGRATION

- How successfully will the development be integrated into its setting?

Historic context
- How does the proposal respond to any significant historic references (such as buildings, features, and traditional relationships such as front doors to gardens, and garden walls)?

Distinctiveness
- How does the proposal respond to the area's distinctive character?

Landscape and topography
- How does the proposal respond to the area's natural setting?

Scale and massing
- How does the proposal respond to the different building heights in the area?
- Will different building heights relate well to one another?
- How would heights affect the spaces around them?
- Is there a standard plot size that new buildings should adhere to here?
- Will the scale of buildings be broken down by materials, windows, roofs or other features, where appropriate?

SCALE

- How well will the development relate to human scale and the scale of its surroundings?

LAYOUT

- How much thought and ingenuity have been applied in siting and planning the development?

EXPRESSION AND HONESTY

- Is it important that the development expresses its function or construction?
- How successful is the design in expressing the building's function?
- How honestly does the design reflect the principles of construction?
- Does the design celebrate the construction techniques and materials, or try to hide them?

PROPORTION

- How much thought has been given to the relations between one part of the development and another, between each part and the whole, between solid and void elements of the facade, and between the proposed development and its surroundings?

ORDER

- To what extent will balance, repetition and symmetry contribute to a pleasing sense of order?

MATERIALS

- How positively will the use of materials contribute to the development's function, attractiveness and robustness?

DETAIL

- To what extent does the care and skill of the detailing add to the development's attractiveness and delightfulness?

STYLE

- How does the design use architectural style?

This new house on the edge of Highgate Cemetery, constructed of glass, painted steel and granite, replaces a house built in 1970.

Part C
Qualityreviewer in the planning process

Appraisal in context

The planning application process

Appraisal in context

'Planning is not merely a matter of allocating land for various kinds of development. It is also concerned with... the quality of the physical environment that is produced. What matters is not simply where development takes place: its form is equally important, and the planning system will be judged by the quality of the result it produces.' So wrote the Planning Advisory Group in its 1965 report, which played a major role in reshaping the planning system. Forty-five years later we are at last beginning to understand how to embed that aspiration in every stage of planning.

For every development site or proposal, the planning process offers a series of opportunities to raise the quality of design and to focus on making a successful place. Making the most of them takes determination. There are almost always competing priorities, and often a lack of time, resources or skills. Leadership – political and professional – can be the key to asking the right questions of the local authority's planning process and of each development proposal. Without effective design champions or project champions (whether or not they are called that), priorities other than design may undermine quality.

Throughout the planning process, design champions will need to keep in mind the 10 basic Qualityreviewer questions:

1. What is special about the place?
2. How should policy and guidance be applied?
3. What is the design concept?
4. How significant is the scheme's impact likely to be?
5. What are the design's strengths and weaknesses?
6. Does the design team have the right skills and approach?
7. How can we ensure that the design will be well executed?
8. Is the scheme likely to be well managed and maintained?
9. Do we need more information and advice?
10. Is the design good enough?

Qualityreviewer has been created specifically to appraise development proposals, supporting a positive approach to development management. It can also be used at every stage of the planning application process (and more widely in the design process) by any of the participants (see page 100). Local authorities can embed Qualityreviewer into this process by using it as a working method for briefs, appraisals, discussions and reviews.

Clients, agencies and local authorities can use Qualityreviewer

- To structure thinking about the brief for a development proposal

Clients, design teams and local authorities can use Qualityreviewer

- To structure pre-application discussions and public consultation
- To structure design and access statements
- To structure planning applications

Design review panels and design teams can use Qualityreviewer

- To structure the formal process of design review, or to present proposals

Local authorities, agencies and consultees can use Qualityreviewer

- In appraising the design quality of development proposals

Raising standards of design takes time: it is a goal to move towards. Innumerable decisions about development are taken every day which, however large or small they may be, contribute to making places better or worse. Qualityreviewer helps everyone who has a role in the development process to see every step as a chance to get those decisions right.

Streets lined with fencing are usually a symptom of thoughtless placemaking.

PRE-APPLICATION DISCUSSIONS

Discussions between the local authority and the prospective applicant before any application is submitted often provide the best opportunity to raise the quality of design. At that stage the developer is not yet committed to a particular approach, and can modify an initial scheme without unacceptable cost.

The local authority's role is to present an integrated response to the initial proposal, bringing together the views of the full range of relevant departments and interests. Pre-application discussions can also involve statutory consultees and, as government advice recommends, councillors (provided that the rules on probity are observed).

The design and access statement that has to accompany most planning applications will provide a useful agenda for pre-application discussions. Using the structure of Qualityreviewer can ensure that both the pre-application discussions and the design statement focus clearly on design quality.

EFFECTIVE DESIGN AND ACCESS STATEMENTS

A good design statement, whether in draft form at pre-application stage or submitted with the planning application, can be a great help in the process of appraising the development proposal.

The use of Qualityreviewer can streamline the process of preparing and using design and access statements (the written and illustrated reports that are required to accompany many planning applications, known simply as design statements in Scotland).

Any design statement should explain how the site and its setting have been analysed, how design principles have been drawn up in response to these, and how the design has evolved. At present the general standard of design statements is not high. Many are written to fulfil an obligation rather than to communicate. Most are too long and say too little. Few are ever fully read.

A design statement that is structured by Qualityreviewer can be more concise, while communicating effectively what planners, councillors and consultees need to understand about the proposal.

Planning applicants should be encouraged to provide a draft design statement at or before any pre-application discussion with the planners. There may be no point in holding a pre-application meeting if the applicant has not carried out initial appraisals and has not given some thought to the proposal. If such appraisals and thinking have been carried out, outlining them in a concise design statement will not be a burden for the applicant. The better the quality of the design statement, the more likely it is that the local authority will be able to give the applicant useful advice and a speedy decision.

The timber details are meant as a nod to the location in the Scottish highlands and the lampposts as a hint of heritage, but no thought seems to have been given to how the arrangement of the houses might have created a real sense of place.

A design statement accompanying an outline planning application may have less detail, but the essentials must be there. Indeed, the fact that at outline stage the detailed design has not been determined makes it all the more important to explain the appraisals and the design principles.

Communities and Local Government *Circular 01/06: guidance on changes to the development control system* explains (in relation to England), that a design statement should leave room for flexibility by indicating the parameters (maximum and minimum) of possible solutions; a range of heights or densities (for example); an average height or density for the site as a whole; or a range of minimum heights and densities for parts of the site.

The circular specifies that a design statement should explain the development proposal's **use**, **amount**, **layout**, **scale**, **landscaping** and **appearance**. A design statement structured using Qualityreviewer may have sections that correspond to the first eight steps of the Qualityreviewer method (the last two steps relate to appraisal only).

These sections of a design and access statement are likely to cover:

1. What is special about the place
2. How policy and guidance apply
3. The design concept (including **use** and **amount**)
4. The scheme's impact
5. The design principles (including **layout**, **scale**, **landscaping** and **appearance**), expressed in terms of movement and legibility; space and enclosure; mixed uses and tenures; adaptability and resilience; resources and efficiency; and architecture and townscape
6. The design team
7. Implementation
8. Management and maintenance

The network of shared streets, alleys and courts in this development in Kent creates a much more distinctive character than a typical housing scheme.

OUTLINE AND FULL PLANNING APPLICATIONS

Qualityreviewer can be used to appraise both outline and full planning applications. Outline applications allow for a decision on the general principles of how a site can be developed. They are used where an applicant is looking for formal agreement about the amount and nature of development that can take place on a site before preparing a detailed proposal.

Outline permission is granted subject to a condition requiring the subsequent approval of one or more reserved matters. Reserved matters can be aspects of layout (within the development, and its relationship to buildings and spaces beyond it); of scale (the height, width and length of each proposed building in relation to its surroundings); of appearance; of access (to and within the site, and connections to the surrounding area); and of landscaping (the treatment of private and public space). But the most important issues must be dealt with at outline stage.

With an application for outline planning permission, detailed consideration will always be required on the use and amount of development. Even if aspects of layout, scale and access are reserved, an application will still require a basic level of information on these issues in the application. As a minimum, applications should always include information on use; the amount of development proposed for each use; indicative layout; scale parameters (indicating the upper and lower limits for height, width and length of each building); and indicative access points (an area or areas in which the access point or points to the site will be situated).

Homes for Change in Hulme, Manchester, provides homes and workspace around communal gardens. The development is managed by a cooperative.

EXAMPLE: CHAMPIONING QUALITY IN DEVELOPMENT MANAGEMENT

The developer wants to discuss a development proposal. One of the local authority's staff – let us call her the quality champion for this proposal – sees it as her role to help reconcile the developer's own interests with the wide public interest, with the hope of achieving an outcome that is better for both sides than anyone imagined.

The first step is to make sure that the developer understands the site and area, and what policy and guidance apply. The developer's short written record of his conclusions is useful at this stage in discussions with the local authority's officers, and will later become part of the design statement.

The planners ask: what is the design concept? In other words: what's the big idea? The developer explains, and the planners begin to understand how he is thinking. Now they are able to consider the likely impact of the proposed development, and to allocate the local authority's resources of time and skills accordingly. As it happens, this is both a sensitive site and a fairly large development.

Sometimes the local authority's officers discuss a development proposal in its early stages by exchanging written comments or by meeting among themselves to present their individual perspectives. In such exchanges or meetings the highway engineer explains what road widths and radiuses are specified in the regulations; the planner has figures for minimum overlooking distances; the police liaison officer explains which types of layout she objects to on security grounds; and so on. In this case the quality champion calls for a different approach. The officers consider what qualities the development could create for the place, and how each of their own particular skills and perspectives could help to create a place with those qualities. The design qualities set out in Qualityreviewer, and the related questions, are used as a prompt for this.

The officers start by considering movement and legibility. Who will be able to get around most easily and reach their destinations most conveniently? To whom will the development be easily accessible? How will the proposal accommodate existing desire lines for pedestrian movement? How will the proposal promote the use of public transport and cycling? And so on. They ask only those questions that seem relevant, and give the issues the attention that is due according to the proposed scheme's impact and significance. The officers follow on with Qualityreviewer's questions about space and enclosure; mixed uses and tenures; adaptability and resilience; resources and efficiency; and architecture and townscape. It is not an easy discussion. There are some difficult potential conflicts of opinion and professional perspective to resolve. But by the time the planning application is submitted, the officers – and the councillors who have been involved – all feel that the final development scheme will achieve more for the public

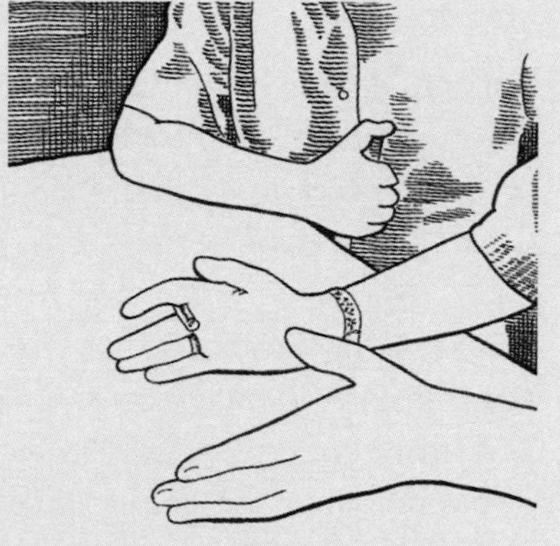

interest than they had thought possible. As for the developer, he sees the planning process as having contributed to his scheme's design quality, rather than having subjected it blindly to a series of unconnected standards, regulations, practices and prejudices.

The developer is used to the job of writing a design statement to accompany a planning application being a chore. This time it is much easier. The design statement has been developing in draft from the start of the project. The site and area appraisal was recorded at the time it was carried out, so now it just has to be accommodated in the design statement. The design principles were carefully thought out as well, so they can now be reproduced in the design statement. This design statement, unlike many others, shows a clear relationship between the appraisal and the design principles, and between the design principles and the final scheme. That constitutes a logical story that the local authority, and anyone else with an interest in the planning application, will find easy to understand.

The planning application process

This table shows how Qualityreviewer can help to streamline the planning application process and raise the design quality of development proposals.

It represents a process that will vary according to the scale of the development and other circumstances. For example, discussions may be held and consultations carried out at several stages, and for major developments there may be formal design review both before and after the application has been submitted.

Who uses Qualityreviewer	Stage in the planning process
Client/developer	Project brief
Client/developer and design team	Initial proposal
	Initial contact
	Initial consultations
Client/developer, design team and local authority	Pre-application discussions
Design team and design review panel	Design review panel
	Revised proposal
Design team	Design and access statement
	Application submitted
	Validation
	Acknowledgement
	Formal consultation
Consultees	Consultees' appraisal
Local authority	Local authority's appraisal
	Clarifications
	Appraisal completed
	Planning decision
	Feedback session

What happens	How Qualityreviewer can help
Project brief prepared using Qualityreviewer, identifying important issues relating to the vision, objectives, design approach and design team (see pages 12–23)	Unless design quality is given high priority in the brief, it is likely to be undermined by other priorities later in the process.
Initial proposal structured using Qualityreviewer. This may be in the form of a draft design statement (see page 96)	This will put the focus on design quality right at the start, providing a set of criteria against which the proposal can later be appraised.
Local authority planning department contacted for advice	
Initial consultations carried out as appropriate	
The client and design team discuss initial appraisals, design principles and proposals with the local authority, using Qualityreviewer to set design priorities. They identify the need for any further specific appraisals (see page 13)	This is the chance for the local authority to focus on what is needed to make a successful place, and how all parties can get the most out of the development opportunity.
Initial proposal submitted to a design review panel, if appropriate, using Qualityreviewer. The design review panel appraises the proposal, also using Qualityreviewer or an equivalent approach	Design review should be a structured and consistent process, giving full consideration to how the proposal will contribute to making a successful place.
Proposal revised (if appropriate) in the light of advice from the local authority and the design review panel	
A design statement prepared for submission with the planning application can be set out on the basis of Qualityreviewer (see page 97). A concise design statement will often be useful even if it is not formally required	An effective design statement will explain the relationship between the proposal and the appraisals and principles on which it is based.
Planning application submitted (either an outline application, leaving reserved matters to be submitted later, or a full application)	
Local authority validates the application and requests any missing documents	
Local authority acknowledges the valid application	
Local authority publicises and consults on the application	
Consultees consider the planning application using Qualityreviewer	The Qualityreviewer approach helps to focus everyone on the essentials.
The local authority appraises the application using Qualityreviewer (see page 28)	Qualityreviewer makes sure that the right questions are asked and the necessary information is obtained.
The local authority requests any necessary clarifications from the applicant	
The local authority completes the appraisal using Qualityreviewer (see page 29)	Qualityreviewer helps to make the most of whatever skills and capabilities are available.
The application is considered by the planning officer (if the decision has been delegated) or the planning committee	Qualityreviewer helps to ensure that a balanced decision is taken in the light of all the relevant design issues, and that these are reflected in any conditions imposed on the planning consent.
The local authority reviews the lessons of any major development proposal about how to raise standards of design, using Qualityreviewer as a prompt	With so many potential obstacles to achieving high standards of design, there will usually be lessons to be learned.

EXAMPLE: A CHANGE OF SCALE IN THE TOWN CENTRE

A professional institute has built a new headquarters for its 300 staff in the town centre of a south London suburb. The building is much bigger than its neighbours in the high street and it backs on to areas of residential housing. The move makes sense for the institute, whose staff and visitors are now much closer to public transport and the town centre's other facilities. Such contrasts in the size of buildings are common where a town centre meets its residential hinterland and where, as in this case, the local authority's planning policy encourages development that is denser and more massive.

The front of the building, facing north, is completely glass, making the offices visible to the street. The rest of the building is clad in brick, with relatively small windows in the sides to reduce solar gain and none at all at the south-facing back, which would otherwise overlook the houses.

Before the planning system was created in the 1940s, the market generally decided how much development would be built on a particular site. Today that is a matter for planning. Is the office building shown here of an appropriate size for the site? Should it be smaller? Or bigger? If the size of its neighbours were the only criterion, the answer would certainly be that it is excessively large. On the other hand, there is a precedent: the site was formerly occupied by a cinema. And the planning authority believes that that consideration is outweighed by the desirability of accommodating more activity, economic and residential growth in a town centre that is very well connected to public transport.

This high street has been blighted over the past 40 years by a series of large buildings, many of which are of the lowest standards of design. Today some large new apartment blocks of little distinctiveness – the tail end of the most recent development boom – are changing the scale of parts of the high street dramatically. The institute's new headquarters, carefully designed both as a workplace and to use relatively little energy, has some attractive features. Unfortunately there is no sign that its plot, size, materials and massing were designed with any consideration of how its presence might have helped to hold the street together visually.

Appraising such a development proposal is made easier if, at an early stage, the local authority has discussed with the applicant the characteristics of the site, the likely impact of the scheme and the appropriate design principles. Qualityreviewer can help with this, providing a framework for both development management and effective appraisal.

The high street is intensifying, but there is no sign of any unifying vision.

Appendix 1
Complementary methods

Qualityreviewer can be used for all types and scales of development, and its step-by-step structure can be used even by people with little background in design. There are several other appraisal methods and services that can be valuable in particular cases. These include:

ATLAS

The independent Advisory Team for Large Planning Applications (ATLAS) advises local authorities on a range of specialisms, including urban design, masterplanning, design coding, transport and engineering. The team is hosted and delivered through the Homes and Communities Agency.
www.atlasplanning.com

BREEAM

BREEAM (BRE Environmental Assessment Method) sets a standard for best practice in sustainable design and describes a building's environmental performance. Specific BREEAM schemes are available for different circumstances. BREEAM Buildings can be used to assess the environmental performance of any type of building (new and existing). There are standard versions of BREEAM for common building types. Less common building types can be assessed against tailored criteria under the Bespoke BREEAM version. BREEAM Communities helps planners and developers to improve, measure and independently certify the sustainability of development proposals at the planning stage.
www.breeam.org

BUILDING FOR LIFE

Building for Life is the national standard for well-designed homes and neighbourhoods. A Building for Life assessment scores the design quality of planned or completed housing developments against 20 criteria. Informal assessments can be done by anyone, but formal assessments may only be carried out by an accredited Building for Life assessor. Several agencies, including the Homes and Communities Agency and many local planning authorities, require a Building for Life assessment as part of their regulations. Local planning authorities are required to carry out Building for Life reviews (for any site with 10 or more new dwellings) as part of the Annual Monitoring Returns that they submit to Communities and Local Government. Building for Life is a partnership between CABE and the Home Builders Federation.
www.buildingforlife.org

CODE FOR SUSTAINABLE HOMES

The Code for Sustainable Homes measures a new home against nine categories of sustainable design, using a star rating system. The code, which is mandatory, sets minimum standards for energy and water use at each level. In England it replaces the EcoHomes scheme. Homes are assessed at design stage and require verification at after completion. Assessments are carried out by licensed assessors.
www.communities.gov.uk

DESIGN QUALITY INDICATOR

The Design Quality Indicator is a toolkit that can be used with all types of building. It has been designed to be used by everyone involved in the construction process from project managers to end users. DQI can be used throughout the life of a building project. There are four versions: the DQI Briefing tool; mid-design assessment; ready for occupation assessment; and in-use assessment. Training is provided for DQI leaders and facilitators. The initiative is managed by the Construction Industry Council.
www.dqi.org.uk

DESIGN REVIEW

Many local planning authorities and development agencies call on design review panels to help them assess design quality. Panels are run by CABE, Architecture and Design Scotland, the Design Commission for Wales and the Northern Ireland Ministerial Advisory Group, and others by regional or local organisations, or in-house. Their advice and comments are generally not binding but may represent material considerations in the planning process.

Design review is not just a matter of showing the design to a group of design experts and getting a correct, expert opinion. The best design review panels are consistent, helpful and constructive. In the past a few panels (mainly local ones) gained a reputation for being inconsistent, unhelpful and divisive. Standards today are generally high, and they are improving.

A design review panel should ask of a development proposal, not whether this is the sort of architecture that the panel members like, but whether the design is a successful result of creative thinking about the type of issues that are considered by Qualityreviewer (which can be used by people with the necessary design knowledge and experience as a basis for design review).
www.cabe.org.uk/publications/design-review-principles-and-practice

SECURED BY DESIGN

Secured by Design focuses on crime prevention at the design, layout and construction stages of homes and commercial premises. It promotes the use of security standards for a wide range of applications and products.
www.securedbydesign.com

Appendix 2

References

By Design: urban design in the planning system – towards better practice, CLG/CABE, www.communities.gov.uk/publications/planningandbuilding/bydesignurban

Capacitycheck, www.capacitycheck.co.uk

Creating Successful Masterplans: a guide for clients, www.cabe.org.uk/publications/creating-successful-masterplans

Design and Access Statements Explained: an Urban Design Group guide, Thomas Telford, www.thomastelford.com/books

Design and Access Statements: how to write, read and use them, www.cabe.org.uk/publications/design-and-access-statements

Design Review: principles and practice, www.cabe.org.uk/publications/design-review-principles-and-practice

Design Reviewed A series of documents on reviewing proposals for various types of development, www.cabe.org.uk

Delivering Great Places to Live, www.buildingforlife.org/publications/delivering-great-places-to-live

Evaluating Housing Proposals Step by Step, www.buildingforlife.org/publications/evaluating-housing-proposals

Inclusion by Design: equality, diversity and the built environment, www.cabe.org.uk/publications/inclusion-by-design

Placecheck, www.placecheck.info

Planning for Place: delivering good design through core strategies, www.cabe.org.uk/publications/planning-for-places

Planning Policy Statement: Planning and Climate Change and *The Planning Response to Climate Change*, CLG.

Protecting Design Quality in Planning, www.cabe.org.uk/publications/protecting-design-quality-in-planning

Spaceshaper, www.cabe.org.uk/public-space/spaceshaper

The Councillors' Companion (2010, forthcoming), www.cabe.org.uk

The Principles of Inclusive Design: they include you, www.cabe.org.uk/publications/the-principles-of-inclusive-design

Urban Design Compendium 1: urban design principles and *Urban Design Compendium 2: delivering quality*, Homes and Communities Agency, www.urbandesigncompendium.co.uk

CABE's programme for sustainable cities is hosted at www.sustainablecities.org.uk